W9-CHB-870

Teaching Power

Teaching Power

by

Calvin E. Harbin

Philosophical Library

New York

PHILOSOPHICAL LIBRARY INC.
15 East 40th Street, New York, N. Y. 10016

Library of Congress Catalog Card No. 67-24574

Printed in the United States of America

Table of Contents

Preface

Great expectations but only modest achievement is the lot of almost all teachers. It will certainly be agreed that soon after entering upon what might reasonably seem to be promising careers, many teachers succeed in succumbing to a mild pessimism concerning both student objectives and achievement. This realization of a brilliant future and a disappointing present both for teachers and students is difficult to rationalize. In the struggle to perform acceptably today, it is easy to lose sight of the tomorrows or long term goals. This dilemma is always possible for pupils, teachers, administrators, and school board members. It is made probable by the competing pressures on all personnel concerned with formal education and the quest for quality.

Recently, voices have been heard demanding merit pay for teachers. To the utter amazement of many, organized teachers themselves opposed this move. Their logic concerned present imperfections in the process of identifying teachers worthy of increased remuneration as a reward for their extra effectiveness. This definitely points up a real weakness in educational psychology, which is the scientific foundation of the art and science of teaching. Few, if any, administrators or researchers have ever succeeded in developing fool-proof formulas for measuring teaching effectiveness in terms of quality or quantity. Perhaps this cannot be accomplished with scientific accuracy at this time. But the need is real, and the situation is urgent. The movement toward a national teachers' examination would appear to be an attempt to insure at least reasonably for what might be described as power to teach. Nothing would seem to guarantee that such power would ever be exerted, however.

This book is an attempt to examine teaching with a view of developing a treatise to bring light to the subject of teaching power, which is, undoubtedly, a complex far beyond teaching competence, teaching effectiveness, teaching ability, and teaching aptitude, though these are certainly requisites or ingredients. It has been an exercise in frustration trying to describe the undefined and to find the missing equation for the term "teaching power." It is a part of the on-going battle for excellence in education. My purpose is to make a contribution. *Animus hominus est anima scripti.*

While it is not easy to tranquilize the professional critics of teaching and teacher education, it is relatively standard procedure for teacher education institutions to "improve" upon their several programs leading to better prepared beginning teachers. This is, of course, a move in the right direction of increasing teaching power for the future and is, in that respect, highly commendable. In this connection, knowledgeable teacher-educators know that there are few if any guide lines for their specialty on which there is general agreement. This would seem to indicate the desirability of increased attention to the study of potential teaching power all along the line.

It is commonly thought that of the three levels of public education in the U. S., their quality is in the reverse order of their ascendance. This may be so. Certainly drop-out calamities, failure statistics, and the national hunger for adult education all point up the importance of strengthened teaching with all possible haste. Then too, the developing nations of the earth are looking toward our country for leadership in their long range planning for their education systems. Teaching power could probably be increased by 20% to 50% by special effort and some talented teachers could very probably improve up to 100%. Just how to go about this dream has not yet found expression though professional teacher organizations, the official education agencies, the foundations, and some university centers are providing a powerful thrust in this direction through their activities. The U. S. government has provided a powerful incentive to schools through legislation, also.

The panorama of historical dissatisfactions with public education includes not only the high cost to taxpayers, but critical emphasis on the curriculum, the methodology, the preparation of teachers, and odious comparisons with certain foreign school enterprises. Previously, as a matter of historical note, the U. S. had been successively preoccupied with English and German education as its models. In all cases, the consideration of financial support has had much to do with the decision on arrangements relating to instructional quality and its over-all excellence. Presumably, the continuing compromises down through the years have been to secure the best possible schooling within the financial competence of the ones who were then paying the bills for education. Education, as the mother of the other professions, is in a position to withhold incalculable good unless its quality and quantity are kept uniformly high according to the standards set by the wisest and best of our citizens.

CALVIN E. HARBIN

Teaching Power

Chapter 1

The Nature and Scope of Teaching Power

American education, from top to bottom, is under pressure to improve. The air is full of all kinds of proposals. Outspoken critics have for several years called for thoroughgoing revisions in the schools' offerings, methodology, programs for preparing teachers, and the basic organization of educational institutions. If one is to believe what has been said and written, the quality of teaching in some schools and colleges leaves much to be desired. This is true in spite of the fact that never before in the history of our country have educational costs been so high, educational structures so numerous and substantial, and teachers so well-educated and numerous. There are those who claim that it is impossible to provide high quality teaching for masses of learners, but rather that a selective process must be initiated so that the pupils with the highest potential can be matched with teachers of the greatest teaching power.

The professional longing for higher pay for teachers coupled with an insistent plea from the schools' several publics that pay be based on merit rating has focused attention on some aspects of teaching power. While the mainstream of American teachers has unofficially rejected merit rating for seventeen reasons as a specific answer to the demand for higher pay,[1] there are indications that opposition would be substantially reduced if and when some feasible plan for evaluating teaching merit can be developed.

Other considerations lending substance to the growing awareness of teaching strength are the recent developments now assuming the proportions of trends. Among these might be listed such movements described by popular catch phrases as "the rising tide of students," "space age technology," "federal support to schools," "defense and welfare doctrines of education," "technical and professional assistance programs for developing nations," and the "shortage of teachers."

While "teaching power" is not a new term in the technical sense used here, it needs some specific description to indicate its present usage. By the term, admittedly used in a special manner, we mean to imply: ableness, efficacy, ability, potency, capability, talent, efficiency, cogency, competency, force, might, or effectiveness of a teacher to more or less permanently influence pupils through various means such as style, discipline, personnel management and control, subject-matter knowledge, organization and presentation. Types or forms of power exercised will be discussed in Chapter 5.

In a 1962 interim report on the School and University Program for Research and Development issued by Harvard University, the question of quality in education was adjudged and found wanting.

> Throughout the 1950's — to use a medical analogy — the Faculty of Education held continued consultations with schools and colleges on the health of American education. The general diagnosis was that, although numerous American schools at all levels were doing an excellent job, the general tone of the patient's health was far short of what it could be.[2]

If education is to help put the foundation under individual and national daydream houses, the quality of professional service should be good and workmanlike. Most people like their memories of the past, but they like their dreams of the future even better. The preparational reality of the present is an arching bridge to tomorrow and possible greatness. And in all of these thoughts, the powerful teacher — not the average one — is the key person.

The student who "learns" or merely becomes familiar with the subject matter of a course, but who declines to apply or use what he has learned, that is, he has no commitment to action, does not intend to use it, takes the "so what?" attitude, certainly demonstrates an academic sickness and needs help. Therapy is indicated if constant self-examination and acquisition of new knowledge do not lead to changes and heightened activity for improvements. Our society is plagued with many whose will to apply or use learning is open to suspicion. Hopefully even those with their wrong thinking, which is no doubt on the unconscious level, may, with more powerful teaching, find some type of correction or spontaneous remission due to a change in thinking engendered by great teachers. Such teachers through their own force, energy, strength, virtue, capacity, endowment, gifts, vigor, and general power to command, oftentimes have the power to incite, impel, induce, excite, stimulate, impress, and activate students even against their old habits, proclivities and initial will.

On a prophetic note, Gardner has described what appears to be building up in terms of a philosophy for change in educational evaluation.

> There will be an increasing constituency of able and highly trained citizens to express their concern for educational effectiveness and to evaluate levels of excellence in education; thus the schools will enjoy a deeper appreciation and face a sharper challenge than ever before. This will be gratifying to the schools but not necessarily comfortable...[3]

It is no secret that there are differences in the degrees of effectiveness of teacher personnel. Students will so testify and administrators will admit this fact. By observation, by testimony, by pay scales, and other direct and indirect means, the competence and worth of teachers are somehow judged. Whether teachers are born, or made, or both, is beside the point. The fact remains that some are far superior to others. Even the same teacher may either improve or deteriorate over a period of time. And further, it would appear, that upon some pupils in a given class, a teacher could exert powerful positive influence, while at the same time with other pupils in the same class, a negative force or practically no influence at all would be felt.

Teaching efficiency is always indicated by certain permanent outcomes and almost never by performance or achievement of students while still in the classes of teachers whose influence is being evaluated. Perhaps there is no immediate sine qua non of teaching power, for in teaching, power is always potential.

THE CONCEPT OF TEACHING POWER

In each of the learned professions, there is recognition and sometimes publicity for the top people, viz., those who have by various means demonstrated their effectiveness. Through specialization, career planning, research, fortunate experiences combined with natural talents and intellectual capacity, so much growth and development have occurred that this type of individual stands out not only in the general population but also within his own discipline. He may stand head and shoulders above his fellow practitioners.

There is a considerable volume of writing on the subject of quality in education these days. Perhaps it is a sign of the times in which we live that the expanding school enrollments, the educational building programs, and the modifications and revisions of programs all carry with them the germinal idea of "improvement." There is no doubt that many parents desire the "best" schools for their children to attend and the "prestige" colleges for higher education. And it is common knowledge that some of our schools and colleges are "higher" than others in terms of instructional effectiveness or power to change the lives of young people.

While much has been written on the subject of up-grading education and along the lines of constructive criticism, it has usually fallen into the descriptive class and has therefore been quite unfruitful in the long run. The time has come to place the construct of "teaching power" in a central, unambiguous general theory of professional quality or excellence in terms of evaluation of products as well as in the earlier efforts of preparing teachers for the learners of this and future generations.

Teaching power is best understood in general terms as the effect a teacher has on those being taught, and his influence in specific terms, of more or less permanent changes in their knowledge, understandings, skills, behavior, opinions, attitudes, goals, needs, values or appreciations.

Teaching skill and power are related largely to time, place, personnel, discipline, and most of all to the increasing knowledge about the process itself. For, as students of history know, what was at one time, one place, by certain persons, in a given discipline with the current status of knowledge of teaching-learning, considered an excellent performance, we now would doubtless not concede as such at all. At least in the light of our relationships and present status of knowledge, our views would probably be at variance with former views. In a sense, the old saying that "Time makes ancient good uncouth" is descriptive of much in the field of formal education. Such evolutionary swings have led one philosopher-statesman to observe that what was once an evil is now by common practice and consent considered to be a virtue, and what was once a virtue is with some disgust branded as offensive or humorous. The often attacked "lecture" undoubtedly would fall into this classification as it was at one time the finest teaching procedure that could be followed. But look at it now! How far it has fallen, not into disuse, but in its reputed effectiveness! The reason most often advanced for this is that the advent of the printing press made obsolete the need for formal lecturing. In theory, but perhaps not in practice, this seems to be true.

Concern about teaching power at the elementary and secondary level has always been in evidence. The high turn-over of classroom teachers averaging ten per cent a year in many places, the low entering requirements for new teachers, the relatively unsupervised teaching performances of most teachers, the crowded conditions in some areas, the high drop-out rates in some areas, and the low pay of teachers are indicative of possible dissatisfactions with teaching whether from the point of view of parents, board members, pupils, or teachers themselves.

Only a few teachers on the higher level have ever had specific preparation to teach at that level. Many feel an intense allegiance to their disciplines apart from teaching it. This may take the form of research, writing, speaking, or just plain "trying to keep up with recent developments" in the field since obtaining their doctorates or formal education. And then, of course, there are those who tend to relax and forget both their responsibility to be an effective professional teacher with all of the intellectual activity this entails, and to ignore their disciplinary debts giving such familiar but nevertheless rationalized reasons as lack of time, heavy work loads, health, and other plausible excuses.

Good teachers are generally concerned about improving their teaching. They know it is both possible and desirable and indeed imperative to keep up their rating as powerful teachers. And those who seek help in this respect usually find it.

If the foundation of politeness lies in the desire to please others, then the foundation of teaching power lies in the desire to change them. Teaching power in action is the fulfillment of a teacher's intentions. It requires a unique social relationship which basically indicates the style and determines the effectiveness of the endeavor.

The term "teaching power" is another way of indicating instructional effectiveness. In one way or another, each person is a teacher and as such has a teaching power quotient. No one has ever come up with an accurate measure for this ability and perhaps never will. Nevertheless, teaching power is of concern to professional educators and to the leaders of society who are concerned with the quality of formal education.

To increase in one's power to teach is indeed a great accomplishment. Graduate schools of education are engaged in helping prospective teachers obtain maximum development along these lines. Special efforts are being exerted through government, foundations, and institutional research to accelerate the process of improving the quality of teaching. Moreover, some think that human progress and the welfare of mankind hinge on the degree to which the race, largely through its teachers, truly learns lessons from the accumulated knowledge and finds ways and means of applying these learnings promptly.

In a strict juristic or moral sense, there are no true laws of either teaching or learning which, if observed faithfully, will guarantee and insure increased teaching power. If there is no royal road to learning, there most certainly is no such road to teaching. Indeed, reliance upon historical rules, or even the substitution of the more modern approach of the gadget procedures, will most likely lead to unproductive results in the long run. Such rules and gadgets change with the passing years and civilization remembers with blushing memory the fiascos of educational fads and frills of the past.

Since teaching procedures are under constant study and revision, if not vigorous attack, it would seem to behoove teachers for the time being to look upon all formulas for teaching power as indicative and explanatory of what others are doing, not imperative and admonitory for themselves. Every teacher's goal, however, is to help the student learn even if new rules have to be devised and old ones discarded. To this end, an increase in teaching power is a worthy goal of every teacher.

An old American rule of thumb, regulating the conduct of formal education on the local level, holds that the public has a right to specify "what" shall be taught in schools but that the "how" should be left to the teachers themselves, who alone, are competent to make wise decisions along this line. Doubtless the underlying reason for this folk wisdom is, that to create the needed permissive atmosphere for maximal personal teaching power, and thereby for permanent learning progress, the teacher should be given wide latitude in the technical-professional process. This freedom, if properly employed, enables the practitioner to take into careful consideration his own desires, his own strengths, defects, limitations and proved effectiveness as well as the many factors relating to pupils and their peculiar needs. Academic freedom to teach is believed to be a necessary ingredient for maximum teaching power, and basic to students' freedom to learn effectively. With freedom to teach in a powerful way, pupils are not denied the privilege of learning in an expeditious manner.

There seems to be a natural reluctance to discuss teaching methods on the part of those who actually teach. Perhaps it is because there is nothing about which one can boast, and while there may be nothing to hide, comparisons with other teachers on this score are odious even to the most favored practitioner.

Teaching power, whether of an individual or a group, cannot be explained merely in terms of methodological performance, which is admittedly a factor but, perhaps, a much less significant one than commonly believed. Neither is the basis of teaching power the empty esteem of colleagues. Corporate teaching power calls for the abandonment of the "go it alone" attitude and development of efforts to help pupils. This can be described as an educational consortium.

The concept of teaching power necessarily involves what a

teacher *does* and is not confined to what a teacher *is*. It will be noted from a thoughtful study of typical statements of so-called "good teachers" that the emphasis has been placed more or less upon the person rather than on the activities of the teacher as they interact with the activities of pupils. Herbert Spencer believed that the great aim of education was not knowledge but action. In an amazing passage, he inveighs against

> ...the vicious system of rote learning — a system of sacrificing the spirit to the letter. See the results. What with perceptions unnaturally dulled by early thwarting, and a coerced attention to books — what with the mental confusion produced by teaching subjects before they can be understood, and in each of them giving generalizations before the facts of which these are generalizations — what with making the pupil a mere passive recipient of other's ideas, and not in the least leading him to be an active inquirer or self-instructor — and what with taxing the facilities to excess; there are very few minds that become as efficient as they might be. Examinations being once passed, books are laid aside; the greater part of what has been acquired, being unorganized, soon drops out of recollection; what remains is mostly inert — the art of applying knowledge not having been cultivated; and there is but little power either of accurate observation or independent thinking. To all which add, that while much of the information gained is of relatively small value, an immense mass of information of transcendent value is entirely passed over.[4]

A statement composed by representatives of the American people totaling over 1700 leaders from all fields including professional educators has been widely used to indicate descriptively the characteristics of potentially powerful teachers. It answers the question of "Who Is a Good Teacher?"

> A good teacher is one who has an active interest in children and youth; has a broad educational background; is professionally qualified and competent; possesses good physical and mental health; has a good moral character;

manifests a desire for self-improvement; can work constructively with other professional workers, parents and the community; and is proud of teaching as a profession.[5]

An interesting report and commentary on the attempts to identify good teachers was published in 1953 as a working guide for the profession and its lay public in their joint discussion of the problem of identifying good teachers.

> More than a thousand studies have been made in an attempt to identify good teachers and develop tests of professional ability. These studies usually tried to identify the "characteristics" of a good teacher. This proved a fruitless approach since the good teacher exhibits almost exactly the same characteristics as a good lawyer, doctor, or other human being. Attempts to identify the characteristics of failures in teaching foundered on the same rock.[6]

Notwithstanding such pronouncements, writers in the field continue to list broad categories of qualities necessary for success in teaching. A typical list includes intelligence, health, love of children, effective personality, broad interests, enthusiasm, and sound philosophy.

In most if not all of the points made in these statements, it is easy to discover that (1) the basic points made are quite similar from an overall point of view, and (2) in each case, the question of degree looms large in trying to assess relative effectiveness or power. It is also obvious that the statements are based on current activities of the teaching process in an attempt to assess the short-term quality of teaching rather than the more permanent long-term results with which we are ultimately concerned.

One of the most elaborate formulas for outlining the several competencies a teacher should possess is known as the California Statement of Teaching Competence.[7] This statement was widely studied by personnel of teacher education institutions in the 1950's and early 1960's with a view of providing comprehensive pre-service preparation in each of the areas of responsibility. Beyond providing for the learning of students, the competent teacher is to counsel and guide students wisely, aid students to understand and appreciate our cultural heritage, and on a personal level, participate effectively in the activities of the school, assist in maintaining good relations between the school and the rest of the community, and generally speaking, work on a professional level. The statement outlines the above competencies in great detail for teachers with from three to five years of experience. For prospective teachers, the "competencies" serve as goals to be reached through "intensive study and persistent effort."

The most significant problem faced by schools at mid-century was in having a shortage of capable teachers for an increasing student population. The alternatives were fairly clear to most of the educational leaders of the time. The possibility of limiting enrollments was considered and discarded by most public institutions as unlawful and un-American. The next alternative was to find enough qualified teachers and resolve the situation in this manner. However, due mainly to prevailing economic conditions, even after degrees were conferred on sizeable numbers of prospective teachers, the percentage of them actually entering teaching steadily declined. The third choice was to take the growing enrollments and enlarge the classes of older teachers, hiring such as could be prevailed upon to accept teaching positions, and reluctantly noting the possible decline in the quality of education. The last realistic alternative is properly described as a logistical approach and called for changing the methods of teaching and the administrative arrangements to make teaching and learning more productive both in terms of the quality and quantity.

Among the factors related to and in most cases contributing to teaching effectiveness are the following seven:

1. The particular style employed by the teacher.
2. Experiential knowledge of and ability to prepare subject matter for use with groups of learners.
3. Ability to communicate efficiently and effectively.
4. Ability to manage, motivate, discipline, and control a group of learners.
5. Display of personality, poise, and fairness in human relationships.

6. Knowing exactly the teaching-learning destination and having courage to embark upon a direct route to the goal.
7. A keen understanding of the general nature of learners with special attention to individual problem awareness.

Each of the above will be discussed briefly in an attempt to explain the nature of teaching power as judged from exterior evidences.

1. *The Particular Style Employed by the Teacher*

By teaching style we mean the manner in which an instructor conducts his classes, the methods employed, the skill with which activities are made an integral part of the teaching-learning process and the over-all pattern of instruction. Just as no two human beings are identical, so it is believed that instructional styles differ from teacher to teacher — *and that they should.* Young teachers should be encouraged to develop their own unique teaching styles to exploit strengths and avoid personal weaknesses or defects.

More experienced teachers are to be cherished because of their style. No one should doubt that the style itself though considered not substantive in nature — only adjective — makes a direct and colorful contribution to the end-product. The style is a part of the carrier situation through which the ingredients of power are brought to bear on the learner. As such, it corresponds to frosting on a cake. Style is useful in making palatable the ingredients of learning.

2. *Experiential Knowledge of and Ability to Prepare Subject Matter for Use with Groups of Learners*

Important contributing factors to teaching power are experience and ability in selecting subject matter to match the needs of learners. Organization of subject matter should fit the probable priorities inherent in the situation. At all times it should be remembered that it isn't the subject matter per se that is important in the long run, but that it is merely used as a means to an end — the end of satisfying both potential and actual human needs. But what is subject matter? In this context it would consist of all the rules, facts, ideas, laws, ideals, theories, and other pieces of information with which human beings solve their problems — whether a teacher follows Pope's advice[8] or adheres to the direct approach to learning, his means is classified as subject matter, and is designed to meet a human hunger either now or later on, but preferably now *and* later on.

3. *Ability to Communicate Efficiently and Effectively*

Verbal and non-verbal communications loom large as ingredients of teacher effectiveness. Here, the part of teaching which most nearly approaches art, comes into prominence. The effective teacher neither says too little nor too much, either in presenting content or in the directions relating to the substantial assignments. Such is necessary to avoid charges of obscurity or the equally inappropriate practice of "spoon feeding."

The powerful teacher can make each student feel that the teacher is talking with him. The quality of impersonality is largely absent in the instructional process when pupils personalize the words and actions of the teacher. While perspicuity is desirable in each direction of two-way communication, it is absolutely essential that a teacher be understood if a high degree of power is to be developed.

4. *Ability to Manage, Motivate, Discipline, and Control a Group of Learners*

The effective teacher is the acknowledged leader of the group. As such, the responsibilities of general management, directional control, orderly discipline, and necessary motivation all fall under his jurisdiction. The teaching force required ab initio leads through personality changes to the desirable goals of instruction which in turn become progress markers to more advanced purposes. It is nothing short of marvelous management when a teacher can insure order among his pupils which is proximately conducive to learning. Pupils become disciples in such an atmosphere which accentuates motivation. Thus, through force of good general management during the teaching-learning period, the power of the teacher can hopefully be extended through lifetimes of pupil influence.

These teacher abilities are the sine qua non of powerful teaching.

5. *Display of Personality, Poise, and Fairness in Human Relationships*

In the appropriate patterns of behavior, teachers who seek to develop strength as leaders with their pupils have only to await opportunities to build solid foundations for their own effectiveness. Pupils seek strength of personality, fairness in interpersonal relations, and the security of poise in their leader. Flaws inherent or deteriorating situations are usually exploited without mercy by pupils. If ever a person was called upon to emote a teacher is strategically emoting personality with every gesture, every word and every step.

6. *Knowing Exactly the Teaching-Learning Destination and Having Courage to Embark upon a Direct Route to the Goal*

The teacher who is not thoroughly sure of aims or goals and announces them to his pupils is in a precarious position. He is much like a ship's captain departing port with a full complement of passengers whose destinations are unannounced and indeed unknown to any of them or the captain. The wasted motion, costly procedures, embarrassing situations, and purposeless assignments to say nothing of fictitious "tests" and empty "progress" reports all would seem to indicate a lack of teaching power. The effective teacher abhors all such pseudo-instructional moves in favor of definite knowledge by all concerned of teaching-learning objectives with a prompt, direct attack on them with full support of all pupils. Courage on the part of the teacher inspires confidence in pupils of ultimately and actually achieving the announced goals with teacher leadership.

7. *A Keen Understanding of the General Nature of the Learners with Special Attention to Individual Problem Awareness*

This point often separates the effective teacher from the ineffective one who has not bothered to inform himself carefully enough. Without such understanding, the so-called "teacher" is a masquerader playing the hypocrite either through ignorance, laziness, or both. The hit-or-miss system of teaching is an abomination. If a teacher is prevented from obtaining a good understanding of his pupils by reason of their large numbers, or his heavy workload, then to that extent, his teaching power will suffer. Assuming teaching power potential, then developing the basic understanding of pupils is the very first step toward realizing the actual power. Teaching power, really the production of intended results, proceeds from this understanding on to more or less permanent influence.

POTENTIALITY OF POWER

When power is analyzed, just as in other areas, we can differentiate between the potentiality and actuality with the possibility of their being co-exclusive in practice, yet in reality, two phases of the same on-going creative process.

Potential teaching power is to its actuality what the bud is to the blossom. Given the proper conditions, the bloom is forthcoming in due time.

The term "teaching power" signifies a process that has two dimensions. The process thrives on supporting responses from students but vanishes when such responses fail. That it is directly sensitive to and responsive to student needs cannot be denied. In this sense it is more relevant to the future than it is to the past. Its thrust is from the present to the future with dynamic quality of progress. Power can never be wholly demonstrated as its potentiality presages changes which continue through lifetimes to come. It differs from control which is truly a matter for the present and the past whereas power is always potential.

BASIS OF TEACHING POWER

From the legalistic standpoint, the power of school administrators originates in the law of the political subdivisions and comes down through levels of decentralized jurisdiction. Not so the power of a classroom teacher who is acknowledged to stand in the place of parents. Clothed with the responsibilities and powers of parents, classroom teachers enjoy a unique relationship with their pupils which becomes the real basis of teaching power. Just as parents have natural capacities in dealing with their offspring which ordinarily lead to various types of rewards, occasional corrections, behavioral control, and other particular ties, so have teachers inherited opportunities for close relationships with their pupils.

It should be pointed out that to the extent such powers are exercised and the relationships understood by either teachers or parents, the strength of such *drives* are indicative of the amount and degree of the *current* power development.

The bases of teaching power are not physical size, wealth, or social position, though these may be used as instruments of power. The power process leading to accentuation is one of give and take or according to Lasswell: "It is cue-giving and cue-taking in a continuing spiral of interaction."[9]

The concept of teaching power refers to observable outcomes in the lives of pupils. These outcomes are conditioned by multiple factors which would probably not have produced such changes without being precipitated by the teaching ingredient. This catalyst becomes, then, the sine qua non of an underlying power potential. The manifestations of teaching power potentiality require time and space to develop. The lapse of months, years, or centuries does not rob teachers of their influence.

Thus the teacher who lived long before the learner did, has, by the pedagogical magic of recorded messages, invited a teacher-pupil relationship with performance on the teacher's part fully performed. Acceptance by the pupil learner completes the arrangement. It is the privilege of some contemporary teachers to make the introductions of our children and youth of today to the sages of history and thus forge the first links of the chain of a relationship from which all manner of grave consequences shall come. Thus, Plato is still in a posture of power as surely as if he were walking in his garden with avid pupils following in his footsteps. For the questions he posed still relate themselves to us and our times. Likewise, communications of a great religious leader enable us to have communion with him as our teacher and to permit him to exert great influence and power over us with many centuries intervening between our eras.

Learning comes in leaps and laughter lights the way when there develops between leaders and the led the bond of fidelity. Given this relationship, great things begin to occur, but not by accident. For implicit in the situation is the purpose of each, blended into united efforts, devoted to helping the learner help himself.

Furthermore, the pupil is deliberately making himself amenable to the influence of the teacher in various ways. Among these are attending to his organized thought, carrying out his assignments, submitting to his tests, participating in learning experiences contrived for shaping specific behavior.

This relationship, which is the basis of teaching power, is active in two ways. First, it is the teacher, out of a sense of dedication, responsibility, and duty who devotes endless hours to the specific task of learning what the pupil needs and what his problems are both generally and specifically; secondly, he is continuously locating instructional materials, exposing pupils to carrier situations, evaluating student behavioral responses, adjusting instruction and retesting as well as recording outcomes. In each facet of the process, a relationship may be developed, which, taken all together, combine into a basis of teaching power. Such a foundation may be further enhanced or it may deteriorate in time, depending upon how well it was built and the subsequent experiences of both teacher and pupil.

Then learning, as a process, calls for action on the part of the pupil with equal devotion to the satisfaction of present needs, solution or resolutions of problems, and the endless quest for cognition. The hunger and thirst of a scholar is never entirely quenched, and like the food and drink for bodily sustenance, yesterday's delights become memories in the face of the pressing demands of the eternal present.

Thus, it is truly related that a teacher's influence never ends but goes on forever. It goes on in the form of foundations in the realm of positive and negative influences unrecognizable in their applications, and in the ideas transmitted to learners to be used even down through posterity.

POSTURES OF TEACHING POWER

Not yet well understood the philosophy of teaching power is beginning to emerge from the sociology of crowds, of events, of personalities, of classes, of men, and from society itself. One of the most striking lessons on incipient teaching power, still in the stage of force, can be read into the physical behavior of the teacher aside from verbal communications.

Canetti, in distinguishing between power and force, claims that the former has "a certain extension in space and time," while "the word 'force' suggests something close and immediate in its effect, something more directly compelling than power." He also alleges that:

> When force gives itself time to operate, it becomes power; but when the moment of crisis arrives, the moment of irrevocable decision, it reverts to being pure force. Power is more general and operates over a wider space than force; it includes much more, but is less dynamic. It is more ceremonious and even has a certain measure of patience.[10]

In military terms, there is significance in a country's defense posture or stance. Observers can derive meaningful generalizations from the silent configurations which at least signify some degree of readiness for action. Closer home, the table seating arrangement by a hostess is based on her understanding of the degrees of power possessed by the guests and diners. Translated to the classroom or learning space, the postures of teaching power are indicated by the following:

1. Sitting at a table around which students sit.
2. Standing while students sit.
3. A seminar room with the teacher as the center of attention at the lower level.
4. Walking among students as they study.
5. Sitting on a desk while teaching.
6. Sitting or standing on a raised platform.
7. Behind a desk while teaching.
8. Talking from the back of the room.
9. Sitting in a special chair.

10. Sitting on a high stool.
11. Actively gesturing while pupils are still.
12. Eye contact or lack of it.

One could read from the non-verbal communications of a teacher varying degrees of personal security, fear, status, popularity, democracy, autocracy, and forceful action. It is also possible to perceive contempt displayed in a classroom. Developed from the classroom situation as a product of the total environment, is the relationship which was described above as the basis for all teaching power.

The essence of self-motivation and independent study routines would seem to be entering into and completing a relationship by a learner with teachers at an earlier time and with earlier proffered communications.

THE COMPONENTS OF TEACHING POWER

It is only natural for a good teacher to select power opportunities of normal situations in preference to other opportunities. Lasswell, in describing the political type, has reported that:

> As such a person moves from infancy through maturity, he becomes progressively disposed to respond to the power-shaping and power-sharing possibilities of each situation in which he finds himself.[11]

Thus teachers, who have spent most of their lives as pupils, come to their teaching tasks with wide experience in teaching power and influences. Such power is not really wielded by an individual but is a collective quantity combining the negatives and positives from many situations and teachers into a driving, forceful influence. Some of the components of teaching power are listed below with brief comments and questions.

1. *Speed with which teaching-learning is accomplished*

A learning task is shortened considerably with the help of a competent teacher. Errors can be detected readily and corrective measures taken to overcome them. By working together, the teacher and the student can cooperate in adjusting the rate of accomplishment to the capacity of the learner. The direct approach to learning can be employed to save much valuable time. Powerful teaching acts catalytically in speeding up the learning process. The vision of the teacher coupled with various other understandings, can be utilized in the process of learning to the distinct advantage of the learner.

2. *Degree of learning, i. e., the amount*

The teacher who arranges the environment for maximum learning is demonstrating potential teaching power. The intelligent use of time, facilities, and materials go far in insuring desired results. Always, the amount of learning is a reflection on the amount of teaching. Just as "the proof of the pudding is in the eating thereof" so too, the teaching power component is evidenced by the degree of learning.

3. *Quality of learning: up-to-dateness, research, universality*

An examination of the quality of learning should reveal much about the power of the teacher. In addition to how quickly it was acquired and the total amount of learning, qualitative facets may be checked to ascertain whether the new learning is up-to-date or dated; research-based or not; more or less permanent or of fleeting significance; the attitude and appreciation of the new acquisition; the desire to continue along the same line and direction.

One definite point to be checked should relate to the ability of the learner to "use" (in the broad sense) what he has learned. This application phase throws much light on the genuineness of the learning and reveals a universal component of the teacher's power to teach effectively. For the powerful teacher's primary aim is to clarify needs and rouse pupils to actions which give dynamic form to realistic achievement.

4. *Pleasantness, smoothness, and skill of operation: friendliness, sugar-coating technique, mother tactics, rough tactics*

Teaching power has many aids to employ in attainment of its objectives. Just as personalities differ, and a person's mood changes from time to time, it is not strange that the effective teacher must shift techniques to fit the occasion. The end justifies to some extent the procedures, no doubt, and the learner must be willing to accept the cost of success of the teaching-learning enterprise whatever it may be. Whether pleasant and smooth, or rough and disagreeable, the principals in the enterprise should understand and agree in advance upon the desirability and necessity of *results* which come from powerful teaching and learning.

5. *Permanency of learning: power to retain*

Testimonials from students of powerful teachers indicate that one ingredient of the teacher's instruction was the resulting permanency of learning. The power to retain understanding, skills, attitudes, appreciations, and even bits of knowledge is a direct reflection on the instructional-learning process with which such products of learning were acquired. Permanency of learning is certainly a mark of teaching power.

6. *Numbers that can be simultaneously taught*

It is not clear whether the most powerful teachers work their magic in the 1:1 ratio of private conferences or in the 1:1 ratio of huge assemblages. Considering television instruction, with possibilities in terms of millions of unseen viewers, one might denigrate the power of such a teacher only to find amazing results. Institutions engaged in formal educational endeavors have generally set limitations in the number of pupils a teacher can or should instruct at one time. From the 25 to 30 in the public schools to both larger and smaller numbers in collegiate and graduate classes, the standards vary around the country. One result is desired, however, by all concerned, and that result *is the most powerful teaching possible.* Restrictive rules on numbers are attempts to insure the probability of effectiveness within the *community* with the wholehearted cooperation of all concerned.

7. *Teacher reputation as a re-enforcing factor*

The fact that the teacher becomes an accepted authority in the eyes of the pupils is one component of teaching power. On the strength of pupil acceptance, usually without much of a question, the instruction assumes dimensions of effectiveness almost immediately and such will oftentimes linger over the years to be cherished and serve as a guiding beacon through a lifetime. The reputation of a teacher, if favorable, tends to accentuate his teaching power.

8. *Ability to size up a situation and use feedback.*
One necessary component of teaching power is the ability of a teacher to utilize feedback promptly and intelligently. In sizing up a teaching-learning situation and taking the indicated measures to enhance learning, the teacher is demonstrating potential power. Given student willingness or a receptiveness to profit from such instruction, the result will be forthcoming in terms of constant, active, alert use of cues supplied by the teacher. While the basis of teaching power is actually to be found in the teacher-pupil relationship, the application of the feedback principle is both a promise and evidence of powerful teaching.

9. *Communication abilities*
Perspicuity is a quality of effective teaching. Some of the worst teaching situations result from confusion on the part of learners in what a teacher says or does and what he actually meant. For pupils are quick to size up a teacher and to adjudge accurately between relative strengths of his verbal and non-verbal communications. To speak with a single voice, to converse so that no one misunderstands, so that every listener surely realizes the import of the message is a component of teaching power of the first importance. The teacher who truly communicates with his pupils is in a good position to exert his influence to a maximum degree.

10. *Personal appearance and habits*
Striking appearance gives color to a teacher's image in the view of pupils. The unusual eyes, strong facial features, height, weight, sound of voice, or some other feature may set off as distinctive a teacher and mark him as one who is destined to be remembered and followed one way or another in the years to come. The

classroom manner, impressive or unusual, sometimes helps lift an otherwise casual teaching situation to positions of continuing prominence and power.

11. *Out of classroom conduct*

The teacher who can successfully demonstrate that he can not only teach but can actually perform in an out-of-school environment has provided convincing evidence to his pupils that knowledge is indeed power when used. But the teacher is and should be without power whose deeds belie his words, or who, while "teaching," hints that he is unsure or even doubts the validity or reliability of his "teachings." It is the "sermon in shoes" that naturally points to power in teaching. Far more potent and beyond the words of advice are the countless acts which constitute components of teaching power.

12. *Intellectual capacity and ability and use thereof for pupils*

One prerequisite to a component of teaching power is intellectual capacity and the ability to bring it into full play in the service of pupils. No doubt just having capacity and abilities lead to admiration and respect for teachers, but the placing of such qualities at the disposal of pupils is quite another matter. It is important for pupils to realize the true situation in this respect and to open themselves up to the maximum use of the teacher's experience, judgment, and characteristics if maximum learning power is intended.

13. *Classroom manner*

The powerful teacher may, if he choose, exhibit a classroom manner which is both coldly scientific in its efficiency of operations and warmly artistic in the manner of its management of human relations involved in the enterprise. Neither side of the coin of teaching power is sufficient without the other. The teacher, who, while in the classroom, so deals with the situation that ever afterwards the pupils find help from the experience provided them, has insured his continuing influence and power. It is generally said that a teacher's influence does not end with the course he teaches but extends to eternity. This is truly said of powerful teaching in an affirmative sense and perhaps in negative proportions for ineffective or undesirable teaching.

14. *Inspiration and attachment or identification*

One very significant component of teaching power is the ability of a teacher to inspire a personal interest in and attachment to the teacher or his discipline by his pupils. In a real sense, the pupils develop a psychological ownership of their teacher and through periods of time to come the teacher is theirs to have and to obey. A lifetime of influence is not too much to expect from a brief encounter with a teacher of real power. Realistically, however, it would seem that this influence tends to wane with the passage of time which is indicative of the quality of the power exerted during the brief earlier teaching-learning period.

TYPES OF TEACHING POWER

In all discussions of power, we come again and again to the realization that decisions are influenced by the application of power. Such decisions tend to produce the effects which are observable as changed behavior or conduct. But power operates always on the decision level. Lasswell briefly describes the social process of power usage as a "special kind of policy making." In a general analysis of the power concept and descriptive terms, he writes:

> The degree to which X influences a decision measures the *weight* of the power of X. The *domain* of power is the people affected by it. The *range* is the list of values affected by the decision (a legislature, for instance, can regulate wealth and many other values). The scope of power is the degree to which the individual *range values* are influenced. We may also speak of *base values* when we refer to the use of values to affect one another. Hence power can be a base for wealth, and wealth a base for power.[12]

Hunter believes that "Power is a term to describe the acts of men going about the business of moving other men to act in relation to themselves or in relation to organic or inorganic things."[13]

If this be so, then types of teaching power can be distinguished and provided for our young people. Research in this area appears to be badly needed. For example, observers note that some teachers have a certain type of power to inspire continued application and interest on the part of their pupils. Somehow, someway, they seem to light a tiny interest flame and kindle it well. The teacher with this type of power should be assigned by school administrators to a strategic role in the instructional process with the idea that a carrier situation will develop at an early period in the learner's formal experience. Some mothers and some fathers seem to possess this type of power, which even in spite of formal schooling, is potent enough to carry offspring to new heights for the family.

There is also the type of teaching power which permits the rocket effect to occur in the lives of learners. Opposing the plateau effect of little or no learning progress, there is a type of teaching power which assists in swift movement upward and outward to those who have already profited from the first type of teaching power described above. In a firm combination, these two types of teaching power are able to overcome many learning difficulties and obstacles normally found in the path of learners.

A type of teaching power rarely on display but possessed by many teachers is the power to lead and push their students to levels of personal accomplishment not attainable without the help of the teacher. Many readers will realize that without the application of such teaching power, they would certainly not be where they are today in terms of accomplishments. Contrariwise, this may also account for where many readers are today because their teachers have not had or have not chosen to exercise such power in their behalf.

The technique for exercising teaching power undoubtedly varies from teacher to teacher and from type of power to type of power. At any rate there is an underlying theme or thread passing through all types of power and all techniques employed. Such a theme or thread can best be described as the decision principle either in the present or future sense, either latent or patent, and always touching the interest of the learner and his welfare. In a sense, the operational stage of the application of teaching power constitutes only the prologue, whereas, in the future, depending upon the type of power exerted, the investment will come to fruition.

THE SOURCES OF TEACHING POWER

What is the source of a teacher's power to influence his pupils? In the main, this power stems from dominant leadership, personality, preparation, readiness of pupils, the prevailing social climate, and the firm desire to exert substantial influence on students. One can readily see that there must be thousands of possible combinations of these factors in a given class. Since such characteristics and qualities cover both the teacher and the pupils, it is not strange that when one seeks for specific or definite data it is necessary to look at the one-to-one ratio of teacher-pupil rather than to the 1:30 situation. This is made necessary by the divergent backgrounds of pupils in a given class and the almost accidental meshing of pupil factors with teacher factors at a given time and place.

Before the American Revolutionary War, Sir William Blackstone in his famous Commentaries on the Law of England explained the legal source of a teacher's power over children.

> The legal power of a father, for a mother, as such is entitled to no power, but only to reverence and respect; the power of a father, I say, over the persons of his children ceases at the age of twenty-one: which the law has established, as some must necessarily to be established, when the empire of the father, or other guardian, gives place to the empire of reason. Yet, till that age arrives, this empire of the father continues even after his death; for he may by his will appoint a guardian to his children. He may also delegate part of his parental authority, during his life, to the tutor or schoolmaster of his child; who is then in loco parentis, and has such a portion of the power of the parent committed to his charge, viz.: that of restraint and correction, as may be necessary to answer the purposes for which he is employed.[14]

It is not possible to say that sex of a teacher has any over-all innate merit to indicate that, for example, men teachers inherently possess more power than women teachers. For both men and women teachers are known to be powerful under certain circumstances.

Neither can it be supposed that blue blood, family or personal wealth, political or religious affiliation, nor other such factors can be considered as sources of teaching power for they most certainly are not. To be powerful, prospective teachers should certainly start off with dominant leadership personalities, the best of pre-service preparation, and an intense desire to exert substantial and lasting influence on their students. To be assured of probable success then, it would be wise to pre-select the social climate for professional practice where all factors seem to be favorable for exerting teaching power including the readiness and desire on the part of prospective pupils. Such an utopian situation may never exist in actuality but the theory is useful in deciding on locations and possible evaluation of probable success.

POWER OF THE GREAT TEACHER

Great teachers live on and on in the lives of others through the transmission of their ideas which never seem to fade away. These living ideas and the practices they inspire continue to be described down through the ages. Assuming the proportions of true classics, their works become immortal. Quotations tend to help keep alive the words of our most influential teachers from Plato through the succeeding twenty-three and a half centuries.

Mark Hopkins, forever immortalized by his pupil who became president of the United States, was esteemed to be a more powerful force than the materialistic factors in the education of President Garfield who is reported to have said:

> Give me a log hut, with only a simple bench, Mark Hopkins on one end and I on the other, and you may have the buildings, apparatus, and libraries without him.

Bell's advice given over forty years ago on the subject of powerful teaching and learning is still sound.

> It ought to be to everyone an axiom, that secondhand

> knowledge is never knowledge. The student should be shown how to do his own work, make his own investigations, perform his own experiments, arrive at his own conclusions, think his own thoughts, acquire his own knowledge. The proper function of faculties is not to teach, in the old-fashioned sense of that word, but to be around handily available, for students to use. Instructors may teach men how to work but they must not do their work for them.[15]

An interesting and yet curious approach to great teaching has come from Canada. Jennings is probably correct in his conclusions.

> The great teacher may "burn to be of use," or he may be neutral about the whole affair. He may be lazy, arrogant, and sloppy, about his person, or a dandy. He probably will be a master of his subject. He undoubtedly will possess some unique skills in writing, speech, research, and the "fair seduction of young minds." But however his better or poorer qualities are arranged, he will be, in the sum of his character, sui generis. A Mark Hopkins happens only once. There are never two Goldschmidts.[16]

In analytical terms, the great American orator and statesman, Daniel Webster, discussed the differences between knowledge and education. In the sense of his analysis, powerful teaching leads to "true education."

> Knowledge does not comprise all that is centered in the larger term of education. The feelings must be disciplined; the passions must be restrained. True and worthy motives must be inspired. A profound religious experience must be enjoyed and pure morality is to be inculcated under all circumstances. All this is comprised in a true education.[17]

Of all the commentaries on powerful teaching, none comes closer to describing the miracle itself than the passage from the recent book by Harvard's President Nathan M. Pusey. In language that sings as poetry, the writer has caught the spirit of powerful teaching much as the prophet called on his audience to be not merely "hearers" but "doers" of his words.

Education begins to do its full work only when the materials of learning, ably and imaginatively presented, penetrate into the very marrow of the learner and set up there a process of desiring that will not be stilled. When the impact of the thing learned, bursting into the self and filling it with excited awareness of the far-reaching implications in the thing studied, engenders a thrilling realization that the self really matters, and urges on irresistibly to new effort, education of the deepest kind is taking place. It is the awesome power of the great teacher, who must himself have had such experience, to work this kind of magic. But within limitations of degree all teachers are under responsibility to insure that there be a minimum of what Whitehead called inertness in the transmission of ideas.[18]

Chapter 2

Teaching Power Indicators and Ingredients

The powerful teacher works diligently to rescue his pupils from mere contemporaneity by bringing to life their historical heritage, their present opportunities and responsibilities, as well as their obligations to the future. It must be remembered that he is not alone in this attempt, but that he is acting as an agent of society. Backing him with divers types of support are the various publics usually described by the term "patrons." At his best, the teacher, to be effective in the long run, must be a co-ordinator of the educational team. Every teammate must assume definite responsibilities for the advancement of educational programs for children and youth. To abdicate responsibilities or to refuse to be a part of the enterprise will sabotage the efforts of those who carry the heavy burden of passing the torch.

Perhaps the greatest of all teaching opportunities comes to a teacher as he arranges conditions so that his pupils direct and release their energies toward worthwhile, pre-selected goals. This is the essence of the Brigg's golden rules of education which summarize the teacher's work as teaching "pupils to do better the desirable things that they will do anyway" along with revealing "higher activities" and making "them both desired and maximally possible."[1] In a very real sense, the degree of meaningful pupil involement is an indication of the degree of teaching power.

Growing in the power to teach means increasing in usefulness to pupils. There is some thinking that the professional teacher has several major roles to play in terms of becoming highly proficient.[2] These categories of service to learners cannot be minimized. Weisse, a high school principal, in a summary fashion lists the areas of teaching in this way:

> An effective teacher must be a play director, an actor, a confidant, an effective public speaker, a technician, a guidance counselor, a record keeper, a critic, a judge, a friend, and a person with a sound general education.[3]

In this connection, it will be recalled that for specific help with learning problems, society has evolved definite arrangements. These are indicated by the names we assign to the methodology involved. Different facets of desire to bring effective instruction to bear on learning needs and problems are reflected in such descriptive instructional terms as coach, tutor, preceptor, technician, intern, apprentice, mentor, proctor, and aide. Teaching power is easily detected in areas of difficult but socially useful learning where the aid of a teacher is the sine qua non of learning such as a very difficult foreign language.

Another important clue to teaching power is the continued thirst for broader experiences which bring new depth and scope to the teacher. This is evidenced by planned travel, earning of credits through recognized study, and reading widely, both within and outside of the teacher's field of specialization. Since the teacher is a living example to his student, it behooves him to attend to both of the areas of influence — precept and example.

It is not unreasonable for a person to feed upon a book or two a week if he is charged with transmitting ideas and concepts to others. Communion with the thinkers and writers of the ages without neglecting our contemporaries would seem to be a pre-requisite for teaching power.

In the past, teachers who have been first to use the "newer" techniques have not always been the most influential. Some activity in this area has seemed to approach the "fads and frills" stage and wherever this was so, it vanished without hardly a trace remaining. The fact remains, however, that the experimental attitude, willingness to innovate, and an uncompromising determination to overcome hurdles in the way of teaching and learning have helped identify our best teachers who somehow "get the job done."

Personal qualities which might increase the efficiency of a teacher, but certainly do not positively identify teaching power, are preciseness in communication, consideration for pupils and colleagues, punctuality in keeping appointments, fastidiousness in teaching space arrangements, or for that matter, personal appearance. Examples are plentiful, however, of where one or more of these qualities were present, but teaching power was missing.

School marks of pupils are not generally believed to be accurate indices of teaching power for several possible reasons. Among these are the teacher's proneness to leniency, the numerous pupil factors operating to bring about the results, school tests are not always reliable in their gauging of what has been learned, and then the inability of school procedures to assess the applicability of learned concepts through translation to out-of-school-life behavior. In this connection, the student with high grades might possibly achieve no more than a classmate whose grades were poor. There are also many important factors not under teacher control, which operate over the years after school, which make impossible the assessment of teaching power by a review of academic grades awarded by a teacher.

Of all the clues to teaching power, the one generally picked up and officially noted is that of research and publication. The quality of such endeavors is not always considered. The most significant inconsistency in this arrangement, however, would appear to be the incongruity between classroom teaching and the research and publication postures. If assurance could be had that each complemented the other, there would be little or no concern. The opposite is too often true. The basic conflict poses each against the other so that if teaching is emphasized, the writing suffers with opposite results if research and publication are stressed. This is a dreadful dilemma. Little or no pure research with subsequent publication of findings come from classroom teachers on the elementary and secondary levels. They are too busy teaching. However, the so-called "action research" is oftentimes performed and used at the secondary level. It must be concluded, regretfully, that in most cases, research and publication do not furnish clues to powerful teaching.

There are many teaching power indicators or ingredients which supervisors of instruction are always seeking. In the list below, more than a score of them are mentioned with brief comments accompanying each one. No attempt has been made to arrange them in any hierarchical order. Neither has an attempt been made to declare that the teacher who habitually follows any or all of the characteristics enumerated is a powerful teacher but the presumption is in that direction. At least it can be alleged that the practitioner who measures up to these qualities has prima facie evidence of teaching power and the presumption can only be overcome with conflicting testimony to show otherwise.

1. *Maintaining Relevancy*

The effective teacher does not play the grasshopper — that is, jumping hither and yon — in treating a subject nor ever forget the pre-selected, announced objective which is based on the needs of society, the needs of the individual, or both. As leader of the group, positive assurance from the teacher is constantly needed by students that they are on the right track. In such activities as delivering lectures, demonstrating, selection and assignment of learning activities, great care is to be exercised to insure relevancy. The essence of the great conversation between the famous Greek philosopher-teacher would appear to be that of relevance to universal issues as well as relevance from start to finish in the discussion itself.

Plato's ideas are, in some current situations, relevant to modern problems. A teacher who permits instruction and learning to depart from approved goals which are closely related to recognized needs of pupils is precluding the greatest possible exercise of influence in the lives of his students. He is, in effect, helping them to obtain answers to which they have no felt need, and for which they have not sought. Worse, he may not be able to recognize signs of hunger and impatience with continued postponement of relating their learning endeavors to problems of highest priority in the opinion of students.

2. *Developing Continuity*

Development of continuity in the teaching-learning process is imperative. Starting at the foundation, the effective teacher patiently builds the structure and erects the superstructure. Perhaps for most students, starting with the simple and moving on into the more complex is the preferred pattern. It will be recalled that programmed instruction starts with the known and proceeds through unknown areas building upon each preceding bit of information. Continuous development of understandings in depth and ideas in scope provides evidence of instructional power.

The power to exert enough influence to insure future progress is a critical factor in teaching. Perhaps it is at this point that the real usefulness of teaching is to be judged. Teachers who perceive students applying in a timely, intelligent manner what they have "learned," are in the favorable position of further expediting this educational process by close support in extension of useable knowledge in both the cognitive and affective domains. Exhortations to "use what you have learned" are fine if heeded. The powerful teacher is himself able to develop continuity and to assist his students to work in that direction.

3. *Heightening Interest*

The teacher who can accept whatever student interest there is only as a starting point and find the means of multiplying it while channeling it toward the objectives at hand, has great potential effectiveness. Lack of interest has no doubt been the greatest single stumbling block to learning in the history of mankind. Among all of the initial or preliminary tasks of the successful teacher, none is greater than that of capturing the imagination, adding fuel to the fire, and in legitimate ways heightening whatever interest pupils have for learning.

The whole concept of "preparation" of a student for the formal or informal learning activities is of vital concern to the effective teacher. In one sense, it is but a waste of time to proceed with the organized attempt to teach unless and until the awareness of need is felt, the desire is keen, the willingness to cooperate, the permissiveness turns to some degree of eagerness to solve problems, change attitudes, acquire skills, develop understandings, all of which denote interest.

It is true every teacher is caught on the horns of a dilemma. One pertains to starting instruction with those who have sufficient interest. The other concerns those who can honestly report no interest of a personal nature but who find themselves present in body only. Pupil interest is developed in peculiar ways and sustained in divers manners. It is not appropriate for an effective teacher to bribe, blackmail or otherwise stoop to unethical, unprofessional, inhuman tactics to establish and maintain interest. Genuine interest is a prerequisite for powerful teaching and learning.

4. *Changing Attitudes*

The first thing the effective teacher does for pupils is to check their attitude toward the subject of study. In many, many cases these attitudes will need to be changed in order for teaching and learning to occur. Attitudes of neutrality, of opposition, of faint interest, of falsely based or pseudo-enthusiasm become worthy of the teacher's attention whenever the relationship of pupil-teacher is established. Increasing the pupil's genuine desire to learn in a specific area is a very worthy goal of a teacher. After all, one of the important products of learning is the attitude which remains after the formal teaching-learning process ends. Relatively few situations would seem to permit the teacher to start from absolute neutrality in this respect. Nor can the teacher forget that the pupil's attitude is a key to almost every element of learning power. To learn is to change — change in terms of action based on increased understandings, additional or improved skills, deeper appreciations, and revised or reinforced attitudes.

5. *Developing Relationships*

The teacher who develops lasting friendships, or other more or less permanent relationships of an affirmative nature is doing a great service. Getting the student started, working closely with the pupil in the inefficient stages of learning in the particular area, and cementing progress with security are all characteristics of effective teaching. What a miracle it is for a teacher and his pupils, who may be perfect strangers to him, to build a wholesome entente which bridges the chasm of time and circumstance! Not unlike the master-disciple bond of long ago, this alliance becomes stronger with the progress of the process. It does not, however, end with the close of the formal teaching situation. One wonderful indication of teaching power is revealed by the growing bond between the teacher and the taught. Deteriorating relationships obviously indicate a lessening of the power of the teacher. What has been stated does not imply frequent communications. Actually the instruction during the formal period of teaching may and often does suffice to sustain the relationship over the succeeding months and years—a relationship developed within a relatively short time to such a force that it is effective indefinitely.

6. *Providing Illustrations*

Almost all students profit when a teacher takes time to provide illustrations for points which to students seem obscure at first. Such examples, simple definitions or explanations for complex concepts tend to do just the opposite of what some teachers do so well as they express their progress in terms of "covering the book." They uncover the hidden meanings, clench the main points, suggest practical applications, assist in fixing the idea for permanent retention and prompt recall, and generally adding color and interest to the moment. Apt illustrations are not easy to find nor to make. They are essential, however, to teaching which possesses power. Lively, reasonable, and timely illustrations tie instruction to the lives of learners in such a way that their apperception is heightened, their perception is sharpened, their conception of the idea is enormously improved. Illustrations from the ordinary life situations close to pupils who are familiar with similiar circumstances are appealing and widely useful immediately in many cases.

7. *Causing Identifications*

One teaching power indicator that reveals valuable evidence on the subject of instructional influence is that of pupil identification with the teacher. Taking many overt and covert forms, but in all situations basically the same, this "I'd want to be like him" feeling translates itself into similarities of dress, voice, educational goals, career plans, investment views, reading habits, marriage ideas, religious interests, recreational projects and employment patterns. In many cases this identification is far stronger than that with parents, pastor, or other non-teaching personnel.

8. *Reducing Time*

In various ways, the "good" teacher has the faculty of being able to telescope academic learning tasks, compressing assignments to fit pupil needs which might go unfilled for a much longer period of time without the teacher. This invaluable contribution is possible when the teacher truly understands both general and special pupil needs, knows the helpful possibilities from the great world of potential subject-matter, is able to make intelligent choices of comprehensive blocks of significant subject-matter for prescriptive purposes, is able to open up and uncover true meanings and otherwise apply the race experience to the pupil's individual problems. Through appropriate selectiveness of the learning activities much valuable time can be saved for more profitable use. Finally, it is both possible and desirable for the wise teacher to shorten time used in pupil evaluation (testing) exercises.

9. *Inspiring Application*

The reluctance to start immediate use of learnings as they accrue on a bit by bit basis is not only frustrating to instructors but fatal to further progress in the area. One distinguishing feature of powerful teaching is the attribute of inspiration to effective use and prompt application of new knowledge. Thus, to some extent, the teaching-learning process becomes fruitful rather than an exercise in frustration producing barren results. It is rather pathetic that so much of our so-called learning never reflects itself in our normative way of life. School learning which does not reflect itself in general behavior is rather useless and the teacher has been denied the possibility of becoming truly effective.

10. *Personal Exemplar*

To some pupils, a teacher becomes a "sermon in shoes." To become a disciple or protegé of a teacher is to accept him as the professional example and model. This occurs in many instances without the knowledge of the teacher. It is always a possibility and prudent teachers must prepare in advance for the likely eventuality which, after all, is a mark of highest personal respect and admiration. Exposure of pupils to excellence is one of the better ways of initiating their educational progress. It is also symptomatic of teaching power.

11. *Inserting Humor*

A touch of humor now and then with all kindness and good intent adds zest to teaching. Alert students come to expect clever remarks and to relish them with apparent momentary relief from the serious process of learning. The effective teacher finds proper occasion for adding the carefully chosen pun or joke but is extremely sensitive about offensive material which could cause repercussions so violent as to interfere with the smooth functioning of the process and the relationship.

12. *Developing Perspicuity*

Verbalism is a curse and an abomination in the teaching-learning process. Much wasted time and effort are chargeable to carelessness on the part of a teacher who does not exercise vigilance in ferreting out and destroying this enemy of learning. Clear understanding in depth is the goal of the powerful teacher. Some teachers, however, permit stopping with the merest acquaintance with facts which have not yet yielded useful generalizations or clearly perceived conclusions which may serve as guides to thought, speech, or action. To teach so that no student will misunderstand, so that insights will occur, so that behavior will be favorably revised is the goal of the powerful teacher. His success is measured in terms of the chosen direction and rate of speed his students make in movements toward perspicuity.

13. *Displaying Patience*

Without patience, a teacher cannot generate teaching power. Just as faith carries with it the elements of hope and patience, so teaching involves them also beyond the professional practice of the direct teaching acts themselves. Patience is necessary to permit the translation of theory to practice; to enable a pupil to savor the substance of true education; to provide the proving period of trials leading to success; and to enable the skeptical to "learn by doing" for themselves. Patience is essential in the total teaching process to permit the arrangement of an atmosphere favorable to neophytes which is another way of describing the non-threatening, collation of favorable factors, time-is-right-for testing situation which is usually not present in reality in the classroom except in a very limited or artificial way.

14. *Communicating Effectively*

Beyond words, or hand-outs, or textbooks, there is a language within a teacher's conversation. One voice is saying in words one message while through non-verbal though perfectly clear procedures, a modification or changed message comes through to pupils. Children very soon learn to size up their own parents and teachers and come, to know, through interpretation, what is actually meant beyond or within the oral communication.

15. *Determining Purpose*

Determining purpose is one of the first tasks of a good teacher. The student remark "I don't know what to do and I don't think the teacher does either" was not made about an effective teacher. The good teacher wastes no time or effort but uses the direct approach to identify the objectives so that he will know generally the purpose of the instructions, and know specifically what he is to do. Essentially, the students are obliged to accept the purposes presented by the teacher or propose more appropriate ones themselves. In the ensuing negotiations the compromise arrangement will serve to satisfy the requirements of society plus meeting the educational needs of each individual in the group.

16. *Showing Hardiness*

Boldness to think "it can be done" and courage to try it are ingredients of powerful teaching. Teaching is no easy job. Those who profess to teach and yet appear to follow the line of least resistance, show timidity in executing difficult policy decisions, carrying out instructional plans, and generally wavering before pupil criticisms are not displaying the qualities of great teachers.

17. *Employing Tactics*

In the day-to-day conduct of classroom activities, the wise teacher will use only socially approved teaching tactics, techniques, procedures, and methods. Unorthodox arrangements tend to frighten pupils, destroy confidence in leadership, and otherwise render products of supervised activities ineffective. The pleasant surprise, variety, and change of pace expedients are greatly welcomed by pupils who tire of monotony, routine, and predictable educational means.

Appropriate classroom activities are vastly important for effective teaching and learning. Variation of type or types of learning activities also provides experiences which are relished by students. The powerful teacher is always careful to select and recommend the type of activity which is psychologically sound.[4] To do otherwise, would doom the entire enterprise to failure and decrease the influence of the teacher in the long run.

18. *Perceiving Conditions*

Since exact measurement is obviously out of the question in teaching, some form of evaluation is necessary. The powerful teacher trains himself to evaluate conditions, causes, behavior, needs, problems, and opportunities swiftly — almost at a glance — without loss of time, without fanfare or even in most cases so much as an announcement of what he is doing. The effective teacher engages in the perceptive process which is preliminary to and concurrent with formal instruction. Of course, any impressions or judgments based on such observation are subject to correction as evidence accrues to disprove "facts" on which they were based.

Teacher perceptiveness can be substantially increased. It is to the credit of many good teachers that they have taken the initiative to improve their teaching power this way.

19. *Stabilizing Conduct*

Since all eyes are turned on the teacher, it would appear that his conduct in school and out of school is considered to provide the model for his pupils. If discovery is made of consistency between what the teacher stands for, what he says, and what he does or is, then such knowledge will almost surely have its affirmative influence on his pupils. The opposite would ordinarily be true but in a negative manner. The great teacher has demonstrated his effect on his pupils, who now characteristically credit him with contributions in this field.

20. *Adapting Steadily*

The powerful teacher possesses qualities which, for want of better names, we shall designate adaptability, flexibility, or ordered change in personality and philosophy. He is not a rigid ramrod to break and neither are his students. Through association and leadership, his pupils also become adaptable and flexible with growth potential for concept formation, reformation, and transformation.

The greatest deterrent to learning in the opinion of some is the inordinate fear of the probable consequences. Playing the ostrich is not a mark of intelligence of either the teacher or the pupil. The teaching-learning process calls for humbleness and embraces both honesty and courage. It has been assumed that:

> ...the major inhibitor of learning is the fear on the part of the learner of exposing himself, of opening himself to the possibility of change... It is argued that most teaching situations present too many threats to the individual's self-esteem for him to be able to open himself to change.[5]

Proof that students are changing in basic ways offers presumptive evidence of teaching power which is well-nigh conclusive.

21. *Developing Poise*

While one often hears stories to the contrary, great teachers possess personal qualities of tact, confidence, courtesy, and dependability and they know how to exploit such personal attributes. Not only do they have these things, but they teach their pupils in subtle little ways how to achieve in these areas also. It isn't that any human is a finished product, but that some are more accomplished than others. Great teachers have learned how to make smooth pupil contacts and how to lead from favorable first to successful second steps in the quest for knowledge.

22. *Becoming Literate*

Beyond the field of academic specialization, the teacher who is literate in social, cultural, and economic realms finds valuable opportunities to set patterns of intelligent behavior for pupils. Perhaps when viewed alongside of the central academic objective related to the narrow specialization, the influence of such should be looked upon as peripheral or concomitant. However this may be, the potential power of a teacher would seem to increase as his literacy in his discipline develops.

23. *Developing Faith*

Students sense whether a teacher has faith in the process of education and in the future. The one who, regardless of the past, busily and intelligently uses the present to create a bright future would seem to have a vision of greatness which time could translate to reality for the pupils. The thought that students have a bright future if they get the education necessary for it is certainly an ingredient of teaching power. Such faith is as the nature of a gift from the powerful teacher, a bonus in a sense, and is transmitted silently though effectively to the pupil who is sensitive on this point.

24. *Assuming Leadership*

Society has deliberately chosen an adult to place with the young learner group so that the benefits of more experience, maturity and wise counseling shall be available for the guidance of individual learners. But beyond guidance, one thing above all other indicators of teaching power is the leadership quality in a teacher plus the additional factor of inspiring pupil leadership roles both in contrived and natural situations. A symptom of power is leadership in evidence both on the part of the teacher and the pupils to meet the recognized needs of the latter.

25. *Using Feedback*

Automatic heating and air conditioning plants employ the feedback principle as do automatic building elevators. Changed conditions, past performance, and interferences all call for remedial action based on exact information relayed to the control center. Thus in the case of an automatic furnace, rapid cooling of the atmosphere will trigger a signal to turn on the fire to warm the building. The opposite would be true for the air-conditioning plant. In the case of the automatic elevator, the door locks in place in transit and at other times except when at the right floor level.

Perhaps the one clearest evidence of teaching power is the demonstrated ability to receive, understand, and employ feedback in a prompt revision of the teaching and learning activities. The teacher who invites feedback is clearly in a position to examine the quality of his instruction, and if not thoroughly satisfied, commence action designed to improve it.

26. *Encouraging Seriousness*

The teacher who understands the pupil's true situation will have no inclination for levity. He will encourage the student to think seriously about serious things. The task as understood and accepted will be so enormous that little or no time for the frivolous will be found. As Watkins taught his students, "The direct approach to learning is the best."[6] Just as the army general sees the mission he is expected to accomplish, so the powerful teacher understands his part in the teaching-learning process and plans his moves with great care. Students who do not understand that the teacher is trying to help them help themselves oftentimes look upon a move by their teachers as burdensome and unnecessary. In this day and time, it isn't often that a teacher encounters a learner who is more serious about the business of teaching and learning than the teacher is. It is a joyful occasion when time does not have to be spent in exhorting students to settle down and apply themselves. The powerful teacher, however, finds ways and means of releasing the energy of pupils so that they apply themselves fully and seriously at the present and thus insure a somewhat better future for themselves.

27. *Studies Records of Former Students*

Of all the criteria for measuring teaching success, none seems to be more valid than an assessment of the behavior of former students. Of course, there is the great difficulty in accurately fixing the responsibility for later performances. Causal relationships, proximate causation, and direct influence are rare. Even when the connection is alleged, it would appear to be a question of proof or evidence. No more pitiful passage in professional literature can be found than the following negative assessment by a former teacher:

> I have taught in high school for ten years. During that time I have given assignments, among others, to a murderer, an evangelist, a pugilist, a thief, and an imbecile.
>
> The murderer was a quiet little boy who sat on the front seat and regarded me with pale blue eyes; the evangelist, easily the most popular boy in school, had the lead in the junior play; the pugilist lounged by the window and let loose at intervals a raucous laugh that startled even the geraniums; the thief was a gay-hearted Lothario with a

song on his lips, and the imbecile, a soft-eyed little animal seeking the shadows.

The murderer awaits death in the state penitentiary; the evangelist has lain a year now in the village churchyard; the pugilist lost an eye in a brawl in Hong Kong; the thief, by standing on tiptoe, can see the windows of my room from the county jail, and the once gentle-eyed little moron beats his head against a padded wall in the state asylum.

All of these pupils once sat in my room, sat and looked at me gravely across worn brown desks. I must have been a great help to those pupils — I taught them the rhyming scheme of the Elizabethan sonnet and how to diagram a complex sentence.[7]

It must always be remembered that sole credit can almost never be taken by a single teacher for achievements of former students. At best, team contributions have brought about behavioral changes. To hear some individual teacher discuss the exploits of his former students and advisees, one would think the teacher was entitled to 100% of the credit. There usually is a host of contributors to the success of a person, among which can be found parents, siblings, numerous teachers, friends, co-workers and even sometimes, competitors.

PREDICTING TEACHING POWER

There are no reliable or exact indices for predicting teaching power. Neither pre-service course grades, attendance records, nor expressed desire seem to correlate very well with later teacher effectiveness. Rank order in the graduating class is not always or usually a legitimate guide to subsequent behavior.

The best predictive data are to be gleaned on the job as a teacher commences a career. Display of the qualities described earlier as the indicators and ingredients of teaching power leave no time for making predictions as the chain of events has already started. Naturally, it may be predicted with confidence that what has already come into view will continue and even grow in strength over the years.

THE MEASUREMENT OF TEACHING

Teaching power is not, nor is teaching competency, measured by any of the following:

1. Possession of degrees or credits by the teacher.
2. Teacher appearance.
3. Ability to talk or write.
4. An interesting classroom manner.
5. Uniqueness of subject-matter in question.
6. Academic freedom enjoyed.
7. Favorable opinion of peers.
8. Favorable opinion of students.
9. Application of formal self-rating scales.
10. Tenure, either de facto or de jure.
11. Reputation and publicity.
12. Credit yield of courses taught.
13. Work load assignment.
14. Research record and fame of teacher.

Any of the above factors would not, of themselves, directly or indirectly evidence teaching power. There is always the possibility of confusion on these points. Proponents of specific points of view tend to believe that other things being equal, as they never are, the possession or presence of these factors offers presumptive evidence at least in favor of teaching power, more perhaps from the possibility or probability rather than the actuality. There are those who profess to see that many of the above factors do or should accompany teaching power without going so far as alleging a causal relationship.

SUBSTITUTES FOR TEACHING POWER

In a sense there are no acceptable substitutes or surrogates for real teaching power. There are, however, many cheap, tawdry, wasteful, and self-defeating pinch-hitters or masqueraders which appear to satisfy the surface need for teaching power. Among these are the following:

1. Ill-deserved popularity and notoriety.
2. Entertainment and amusement.

3. Busy work of a meaningless nature.
4. Administrative authority, position, and power.
5. Family name, reputation, or wealth.
6. Assignments of difficulty for difficulty's sake.
7. Low standards so achievement becomes easy and simple.
8. Propaganda and indoctrination.

The forms of indoctrination and propaganda which masquerade for true education are especially self-defeating. The time, effort, and attention required for real teaching power are wasted on the spurious substitutes mentioned above. Parrot-like performances never qualify as true evidences of teaching power. Unless the learning develops as the product of residual remains of meaningful experiences, the counterfeit mark is upon it. If there is no royal road to learning, there definitely is no substitute for teaching power.

Some of the recommended ways of influencing students are suggested below in the picture of a powerful teacher. In a sense, the teacher who follows the suggestions has a good chance of extending his power and influence both on the short term and long range basis. While practically all of the points are descriptive in nature, they also operate as suggestive of power constructs within the limits of all a teacher's activities.

PICTURE OF A POWERFUL TEACHER

1. Is an expert in field only as a resource person for other learners.
2. Is still a student in truth and in fact.
3. Won't tell answers glibly.
4. Assumes responsibility for his own education and suggests that his students take responsibility for getting their own answers.
5. Arranges tough self-discipline to stop relaxation and obedience on part of his students who will take no responsibility on their own but depend on their teacher for everything.
6. Stays out of student's way in learning.

7. Puts emphasis on what students can do, see, think rather than on what the teacher can do, see, or think.
8. Stresses a "seeking together" vs. the words of wisdom approach or preachy type of approach.
9. Assumes the social relationship difference of "fellow students with the teacher only a little more mature" vs. "I am the authority and you are not."
10. Moves from the old concept of "teacher-authority" to the position of the "resource expert" by a logistical manipulation of group dynamics.
11. Is a habitual "sharer" versus "the teller."
12. Generates "trust" versus "fear."
13. Takes the attitude of "You must experience this yourself" versus "My views and experiences are perfectly sufficient for you so don't question them."
14. Arranges two-way communication versus one-way communication.
15. Hardly says anything at times so that anxiety and silence may force persons to take responsibility for their own welfare in learning.
16. Calls on all pupils to emote.
17. Does not do the work of the student for him but confronts his pupils with questions and lets discomfort wreak their toll. This drives the student toward education.
18. Gets the student's attention and holds it.
19. Gets the student's energy and time devoted to selected tasks.
20. Permits and encourages students to discuss the "why and how" in class in order to capture energy and attention.
21. Permits students to air their assumptions about teaching and learning and their personal responsibilities in the the process in order to capture their energy and interest.
22. Attempts to "undo" the undesirable learning that the years and many others have done for a given group.
23. Understands each group and each member of it in terms of present purposes, backgrounds, future plans, external influences, and changing nature of views through a very careful study in depth.

Chapter 3

The Measurement of Teaching Power

There is something fascinating about exploring the unknown, especially if uncovering concepts will help millions of teachers and students to develop more effective instruction. This chapter attempts to present an organized and critical discussion of the subject of teaching evaluation. Education has been vulnerable for centuries because it has not devised equitable and accurate means of measuring teaching power promptly. Although the rules governing teaching power are not yet clearly established, the fact remains that some teachers are more effective than others as judged from simple observation, testimonial of students, reports of supervisors, deans, and principals.

RESPONSIBILITY FOR EVALUATION

When one considers whose job it is to measure teaching power, it becomes apparent very quickly that all those involved in the teaching-learning process do it informally, more or less, from a protective point of view. Officially, the administration and school board or equivalent have primary responsibility in this area. Then department heads, principals, deans, and supervisors work in the area under delegated responsibilities. Informally, fellow teachers quickly size up the stature of their colleagues. In one way or another, oftentimes on the basis of hearsay, students develop an image of a teacher. Then the teacher himself develops a realization or basic understanding of how potent he is in truth and in fact; though, sometimes it is very difficult for the ineffective teacher to accept such an evaluation of his own deficiencies, the human ego being what it is.

Whose job is it to measure teaching power? It is the responsibility of each of those participating in the teaching-learning process to do so. This includes members of the school board and the board itself, the school administrators, the instructional staff and the students. Such evaluation is two fold: checking on what is being learned and how well the subject matter is being taught. But these are all relatively short-term matters requiring constant team work to perform. For the long term approach the students themselves and their lives will testify to the efficiency of their instruction — and by this time, it will be well-nigh impossible to separate many of the contributions or to date their acquisition. Measuring teaching power is a task, however, for society to accomplish in time to reward during the lifetime of the great teacher. Too often such recognition has come too late for those who have enriched the lives of their pupils and fellow citizens.

How do we measure teaching power when no approved technique is currently available for this purpose? We don't "measure" in the strict meaning of the term. It would be more nearly accurate to use "evaluate" to describe the process most often employed by teachers and students alike.

Actually, when a teacher holds forth in a class situation, there is every reason to believe that the instruction may be evoking widely differing reactions on the part of students. In a very real sense, the state of readiness of the learner would seem to govern both the quality and quantity of learning. Among those who are maturationally ready, there may be vast differences in psychological motivations. Even in the highly selective groupings, there is, nevertheless, likely to be a wide range in apperceptive mass, general experiential background, and specific personal interest for the subject of instruction.

Perhaps the above holds the key to impressions of students in the same class, some of whom would honestly classify the session as "a waste of time," while others believe it to have been "terrifically good" as a meeting. There would also be those who would take a position between these extremes. This is so because of the personal or individual experiential differences which are brought to the class by students. Knowledge of such reactions would be of utmost value to the teacher who might promptly employ this "feedback" in further planning for the course to increase its effectiveness with each student. Teaching and learning both require continuous intellectual adjustments in relevant, direct progression toward truth as it is currently glimpsed.

As Garrison rightly says:

> Learning is not a chance matter. Only the extraordinarily able and mature student will do his own learning without a teacher. And at the other extreme, obviously, there are weak students who will never learn even *with a teacher*.[1]

In connection with the evaluation of teacher effectiveness, it might be well to review the accepted measures of teaching power. Unless learning is effectively demonstrated, teaching attempts have not achieved enduring success. Reliance cannot be placed on time-serving activities, popularity, methodology, or even the nature of the subject matter as indices of effectiveness. *The power of ideas at work is the only basis for adjudging teaching power.* Indeed, the acid test of a teacher's success is the extent to which his ideas and their offspring are actualized in the behavior of his students and their students. Recognition of the importance of a professional teacher as an idea specialist is one key to human progress. If the ideas are good enough, and sound teaching is employed, great influences will be exerted on all whose lives are touched by the practicing educator. For it is the teacher more than parents, more than mass media managers, more than government officials, and religious leaders, who has learned how to get and how to weigh the relevant facts on an issue, how to base his judgment on solid foundations, and how to evaluate the sometimes subtle, elusive, and variable factors we call human facts. He is, by virtue of his calling, a worker with race experience and memory plus a knowledge of history. While this work is interesting, it is not for himself alone or for its own sake that he spends endless hours of study and preparation to achieve understandings. The real teacher cannot keep these understandings bottled up within his own life, but must, to be happy and insure peace of mind, share them with his students. In other words, he finds the subject-matter, organizes it, and takes it where it is most needed. His quest is brought to a succcessful conclusion when he finds those who need his help and the ideational products are put to work.

The Freudian concept of creativity has application in the life of an effective teacher. For it is not without foundation to assume that what a teacher is really doing is making life, at least in the sense of making it more abundant, more alive, and more effective by producing changes in students. The powerful teacher helps the student to help himself in many ways, not the least of which is the eradication of interferences to or with making a good life. It is not that the powerful teacher does things to his students as it is that he works with them in a shoulder-to-shoulder attempt to overcome through intelligence the individual and race group problems assigned as a mutual responsibility. In this sense of shared responsibility, joint venture, and common goals, the measure of teaching power is not to be found by looking to the teacher alone. There are too many causal relationships involved for this to be true. The principles of group dynamics, operating as a normal pattern, must be brought into the deliberations. It is here that many teachers stand or fall as powerful influences on pupils. For the ability to provide top management to personnel and thereby manipulate the teaching-learning situation for best results is a real basis of teaching power. Skill in organization for teamwork, skill in obtaining maximum participation of each member of the group, and skill in reducing fear of failure are among the sine qua non of teaching power.

PRODUCTS OF TEACHING POWER

Teaching power should be assessed in terms of student change and growth, specifically in the areas of

1. Thinking effectively
2. Communicating his thoughts clearly
3. Making relevant judgments on basis of facts
4. Discriminating among values
5. Adjusting to changing society

It should be pointed out that teaching power is *not* measured by qualities usually considered desirable for teachers. Among these characteristics are the following:

1. Possession of degrees or credits
2. Appearance
3. Ability to talk or write
4. An interesting classroom manner
5. Uniqueness of subject-matter in question
6. Academic freedom enjoyed
7. Favorable opinion of peers
8. Favorable opinion of students
9. Application of formal self-rating scales
10. Tenure either de facto or de jure
11. Reputation and publicity
12. Credit yield of courses taught
13. Work load assignment
14. Research record and fame

Turner, in a perceptive article, points out that ability to form and use concepts appears to be related to skill in teaching as distinguished from other qualities which would not by themselves render the teacher effective. Among the qualities mentioned which would not insure powerful teaching were:

1. Friendly understanding classroom behavior
2. Responsible, business-like classroom behavior
3. Favorable attitude toward pupils
4. Favorable attitude toward democratic pupil practices
5. Emotional adjustment
6. Stimulating imaginative classroom behavior
7. Traditional vs. permissive points of view[2]

There are, unfortunately, some definite hindrances to measuring teaching power, among which the following are representative:

1. Time lapse or the waiting period for life tests.
2. Causal relationship understandings. Separation of multiple influences leading to power.
3. Processing "clues" regarding effectiveness of a teacher.
4. Weighing short-range and long-range power of teachers.
5. Inability to suitably reward known and demonstrated power thereby making attitude toward measurement less enthusiastic than otherwise.

The confusion and injustice regarding recognition of teaching power including scholarship in connection with instruction is truly amazing. It is possible to be judged in some quarters on bulk or quantity rather than on the more accurate basis of quality or merit. There are, however, no really effective agreed-upon criteria by which teaching may be appraised. There are those who believe that teaching is judged on a hit or miss pattern. Evaluations now and in the past have largely centered around hearsay (which in most societies is considered thoroughly unreliable), brief visitation by superior, student opinion, research and publication, or by the even less relevant area of community service.[3]

Classroom teachers, through their professional organization, issued a statement to the effect that:

> The ultimate criterion of good teaching is pupil progress. Pupils should emerge from school with an adequate assortment of skills and knowledges. They should have desirable attitudes and other attributes of good character. Their habits and knowledge should enable them to preserve and promote their own mental and bodily health and that of others. Pupil progress toward some of the goals of education, although not all, can be accurately measured. However, it is difficult to disentangle the influence of a single teacher from other factors affecting progress.[4]

Writers in the field of school administration find much to say about evaluation of instruction. Typical of the entries on the subject are the following:

> As suggested above, the most important purpose of evaluation is improvement of service. This is the major emphasis that evaluation should receive. This requires some definition of what desirable or outstanding teaching service is as a basis for the evaluation. It is extremely important that teachers participate in the framing of the characteristics of the good or superior teacher. They also must participate in the development of the plan of evaluation.
>
> The success of a program of teacher evaluation can only be judged in light of the purposes. Widely varied or confused

purposes may sharply reduce the value of any program. The assumption is unsound that evaluation for improvement of instruction can be combined with evaluation for purposes of paying teachers in accord with their worth. In fact, evaluation programs that have contributed considerably to the improvement of instruction may be largely destroyed by the threat of payment in accord with the contribution made. The development of the plan of evaluation of teachers should be seen as a cooperative activity involving teachers and other staff. Its purposes must be clearly defined and carefully followed if its potential is to be reasonably well realized.[5]

Along the same line is a passage from Stoops and Rafferty.

Completely objective evaluation is an ideal but unattainable goal. It would be wonderful if some method could be devised whereby a teacher could be evaluated by an electronic brain, or by some mechanical device which would guarantee one hundred per cent accuracy. In the absence of such a deus ex machina, it is necessary for the administrator to adopt one or more of the methods of rating available to him.

. . . .

Once we concede that teaching is an art, it follows that it should be appraised in the same manner that other art forms are judged. This involves criticism parallel in many ways to art criticism, with such areas as color, form, design and message finding their counterparts in the art of teaching. Administrators in the future may find themselves judging the teaching art by its total impact upon the eye and heart of the observer, rather than by counting individual brush strokes or analyzing the chemical composition of paint or canvas.

The profession has not, however, as yet reached this stage in its evolutionary development. Until it does, it will be best to use an arbitrary rating device which will at least have the advantage of including the commonly recognized components of good teaching, arranged in descending order of importance and weighted in accordance with relative significance. In a school district which relies upon unilateral rating, such a card should be simple, brief, and *easily* understood. It should provide for several classroom visits by the supervisory officer at different times of the day over a period of several months. It should assess the totality of the teacher's influence upon his pupils, his colleagues, his administrators, and his community, and should be placed in the teacher's hands in ample time for him to secure maximum benefit from it. If in our present state of professional inadequacy, we must achieve the total only through the adding up of the various parts, then at least let the parts be vital ones. Let them approximate at the end of the rating period a recognizable (if only a one-dimensional) picture of the teacher in his job.[6]

An authority in the field of school supervision also comments on supervision of teaching from the point of view of measuring effectiveness.

> The use of rating scales implies that it is possible to construct a definite yardstick with which to measure the effectiveness of a teacher. There are two important reasons why this cannot be done: (1) the human factors in the teaching situation are all variables, thus forming an impossible base upon which to establish a constant measure; (2) rating scales are composed of many items, and it would be impossible for a teacher to conduct himself in such a manner that they would all be applicable to him on any one day — if more than one day is used the evaluator merely adds variables to the rating situation.[7]

One of the more useful diagnoses of teaching effectiveness through examinations functioning not only to reveal what pupils have learned but also as a reflection of the teacher's power, has been published by Bossing.

> The past 25 years have witnessed a steadily rising emphasis upon evaluating devices that would single out the efficient from the inefficient teacher.
>
> . . . .

For too long, measurement of teaching success has been used for the purpose of promoting, hiring, and firing teachers. From a purely pedagogical standpoint, measurement of teaching effectiveness finds its greatest value in the possibilities it offers for the improvement of teaching. It is not enough to diagnose student difficulties. Many so-called student weaknesses are the result of poor teaching procedures. The teacher should recognize that an examination, properly prepared, may function as a two-edged sword. It reveals the weaknesses of the pupils, and lays bare the shortcomings of the teacher. The examination, if improperly prepared, may reveal in its make-up a lack of any true grasp of the subject taught, the failure to separate the relevant from the irrelevant, an overemphasis on the trivial, a lack of coherence and progression in development, and the predominance of questions which call for a good memory rather than those which are thought provoking. Often an analysis of an examination presents a fair picture of the mental distortions of the teacher with respect to the subject taught.[8]

Variables of Teaching Style

The University of Indiana's Institute of Educational Research of the School of Education has published a list of specific variables used or discussed in the study of teacher effectiveness. The list includes 248 specific variables.

In a scholarly report on the variables of teaching which are measurable to some degree, Allport has provided convincing evidence that teaching activity can indeed be analyzed, but determination of the degree of effectiveness is far more difficult. His list of variables includes the following:

1. Stating the agenda
2. Proportion of time spent in lecturing or expounding
3. Teacher-member centering vs. student-student centering. (Where is the focus of attention: the authority?)
4. Directive vs. non-directive questioning
5. Commendation and acceptance (praise for contributions)
6. Rejection of student ("off the beam" unwelcome remark)

7. Disregard of student (fails to see upraised hands or acknowledge them)
8. Use of blackboard
9. Use of illustrations from everyday life
10. Digressive material. Wide digression and irrelevancy creeping in?
11. Note taking
12. Humor

All of these 12 variables are based on objective measures. The observer counts the number of happenings of a given type during a class period. Three additional variables are recommended, of a more subjective nature, calling for the use of a rating scale. A four-point scale has been found useful for this type of recording.

13. Self-confidence. Many teachers are manifestly ill at ease; others, whatever they may feel inside, give the appearance of poise and self-confidence. Ratings on this variable are relatively reliable.
14. Vocal assertiveness. An over-all rating on this variable seems potentially useful. Some voices are definitely outgoing, some withdrawn. There are, to be sure, subtler variables pertaining to voice quality that might be studied; but for our initial list we shall include only this broad characteristic of vocal habit.
15. General organization of the teaching hour. Over and above the particular features of style included in this list, it seems worthwhile to obtain an over-all rating on the extent to which the instructor carried through a plan of organization in his work for the day. Was the hour well-structured or was it haphazard?[9]

CURRENT SCHOOL CRITERIA FOR MEASUREMENT

Certainly, the items enumerated show differences in style, but doubt is expressed as to whether they show effectiveness or ineffectiveness in teaching. Ultimately the educational value of teaching is generally measured by the criteria applied by observers with these standards:

1. Students' grades
2. Attendance records
3. Student participation
   a. number who recite, ask question, etc.
   b. number who raise hands
   c. number who talk with teacher after class
   d. ratio of participation during each half of class
4. Manifestations of students' interest
   a. occasions of inattentiveness (reading newspapers, etc., napping)
   b. over-all ratings on interest (high, etc.)
   c. indications of hostility (disapproval shown by students)
5. Observers' summary judgment. (weighed and over-all conclusions)[10]

FACETS OF TEACHING POWER

Any realistic assessment of teaching power would of necessity involve studies of its magnitude, its duration, its changing nature, differences in teacher-pupil power relationships, aptitude for teaching power, controls of teaching power, and the effects of rejection of the basic teacher-student relationship by either the teacher or the student. Many variable factors would also need to be studied with their implications for affecting teaching power. Among these might be peer relationships, personal self-esteem, state of maturity, security status, rewards offered and received, publicity attending the teaching-learning process, capacity and aptness for learning and for teaching, as well as the methodology employed and the situation or situations prevailing. By reason of the nature of the subject itself, such studies would necessarily require the historical approach with much emphasis on psychological, sociological, and scientific procedures to complement the findings of the evaluators.

In terms of the facets of teaching power to be measured, we have to consider its magnitude, its duration, its changing nature, the individual differences in the relationship, the aptitude for teaching power, the effect of rejection on the relationship, and the controls ordinarily placed on teaching power. Any realistic assessment of teaching power would take into account not only the above but also consider the various peripheries, such as the environmental factors of teacher, peers, self-image, job security, publicity, and economic rewards.

Magnitude

The magnitude of teaching power relates to its quantity or how much power there is brought to bear on students. It is related to but separate from the following point. In the past, society has had to wait many long years to gain perspective enough to decide this question.

Duration

This relates to the time period over which the power extends and, whether weak or strong, the months and years of influence from a teacher would constitute the durability of his power. The teacher whose power extends no further than the limits of the course is, of course, not influencing his students very much. On the other hand, lessons learned well have continued for 50 years or more with accompanying duration of the teacher's power to substantially influence a former student.

Changing Nature of Power

At first, during the initial period of adjusting, the influence of a teacher over a pupil may be negligible with tendencies to increase as time goes by. On the other hand, the influence may be strong during the course of study and immediately thereafter start to wane and gradually disappear. It is the powerful teacher who can light the little, flickering flame during the formal instructional period which shall ever afterwards grow in size and intensity into a raging fire to endure forever. This is the type of teacher described by Pusey as his great teacher.

Individual Differences

In a given class, many differences among students appear to complicate the process. From the teacher's standpoint, a single action might influence various pupils in totally different ways even in the opposite directions. What appeals to a given student as valuable to him might not even be understood much less esteemed by others. This prevents evaluation of a teacher on a whole-class basis.

Aptitude for Teaching Power

Those who by reason of their natural endowments and who obtain the formal preparation for teaching, have every reason to anticipate success in teaching. While research along the line of predicting teaching success has not been particularly fruitful, aptitude for teaching can certainly be identified before entering upon a career. Even informal studies of activities related to teaching will throw some light on whether a person could teach if he desired to do so. Inventories and psychological value studies reveal, to some extent, aptitude in this area. Much, however, remains to be done.

Rejection

Rejection by either the pupil or the teacher of the other would seem to prevent teaching power even though the putative relationship of teacher-pupil continued over a relatively long period of time. Defeatist in the extreme is the effect of rejection. The one that would influence can't while the one that would be influenced won't permit it to occur. There is the twilight zone of rejection where the decision to reject is not yet complete, and almost unaware to anyone, the influence starts its leavening process. Sometimes the tide is turned, and the tentative rejection becomes tentative acceptance. Through the peculiar ways in which a teacher exerts short term power over pupils, the pupil comes under the power of the teacher. Thus the teacher's ability to perform — which is the essence of teaching power — is already in demonstration.

Controls on Teaching Power

There are many controls on teaching power. Some of the more obvious ones are related to time, manners, intellectual capacity, place, mission, and professional rewards.

Chronological Controls

The limits of time, or administrative scheduling of the year, months, days, and classes all contribute to this type of control. Experimentation along this line is and has been the subject of interest for the past several years. The question is: "Can the influence of a teacher be enhanced by regulating the blocks of time allotted?" Class periods are believed to run from only a few minutes in some elementary schools to all day long in some institutions of higher learning. No doubt, in some segment of school administration, there is the belief that the controls of time are necessary to insure balance and a reasonable chance to attain the goals of the school.

Manners

Courtesy, etiquette, modesty, and the like qualities exert some measure of control on teaching power. Such techniques as the so-called "shock technique" as attention getters might be an illustration of this. Also, many students become extremely reticent in class and thus do not meet the teacher even half way in the complicated process of teaching and learning. Polite scientific impersonality on the part of both teacher and pupil is believed by some to be an essential for teaching power but this certainly needs to be within socially accepted standards. It can be carried too far.

Intellectual Capacity

There is a limit to the amount of influence a teacher can have on pupils who are hindered by their mental capacities. This works in the reverse fashion also. Pupils whose capacities exceed those of their teachers will soon exhaust the amount of helpful influence available to them.

General

In the Edling rationale, there are six areas within each of which there may be practical controls on the powers of the teacher. Among the factors certainly at work within each of the areas of teaching there are those of time, manners, and place, as well as those of intelligence, rewards, and scheduling considerations. His analysis of teaching shows quite clearly that in its broadest concept teaching is far more inclusive than mere instruction. Beginning with the first task of teaching, Edling has indicated the progression as follows:

1. The individual and collective needs of those to be taught must be assessed continuously.
2. In order to attain the objectives of education, there must be continuing preparation of instructional materials (stimuli) to which learners may respond. (Subject matter — selected, organized and assigned)
3. Learners must be exposed to instructional stimuli in ways which optimize the desired learning. (This is instruction)
4. The behavior (responses) of learners must be evaluated constantly for adequacy and appropriateness.
5. Inadequate and inappropriate learner behavior existing after instruction and evaluation must be modified by learning experiences which are unique for the individual.
6. Records must be maintained and reports rendered at periodic intervals.[11]

TESTS OF TEACHING POWER

As Hechinger has indicated, "The crucial test of teaching is what effect it has on those who are being taught." And this effect is not readily discernible even to trained observers. It is not even apparent to the pupils themselves who have not yet lived long enough to gain the perspective so necessary for evaluation of their experiences.

School trials such as tests and examinations reflect to some degree one aspect of teaching power but the real test generally comes as a "life" trial far removed from the teaching process in point of time and personal association. School tests are in the main valid only in school and for some specific academic test, while later life tests are more truly indicative of the value of all experience regardless of how, when or where obtained. The important point is to know and be able to apply knowledge. In this sense, at least, the most powerful teacher is the one who, acting as a catalyst, causes the learner to profit both while in school and throughout his life from the accumulated knowledge and wisdom of mankind as he appropriates it to his own uses.

In a true sense, the acid test of teaching power runs not for a class period, but for the lifetime of the learner. Delayed action of the acquired data, torpedo effects of questions, and continuous reformation of views are in the highest and best tradition of a powerful teacher's lifetime influence on his students.

The practical test of a teacher's power is the subject of a continuing trial with his former and present pupils. The quality of pupil activities may reflect the earlier contributions of their teachers. The short term impact of the teacher in the matters of reward, punishment, and the other areas of pupil influence, may now be echoed in the total outlook of the former pupil as he makes decisions. It is not easy and may be impossible to isolate the influence of a given teacher long after the period of his teaching has passed. It would be more accurate to assess group contributions with all former teachers falling into the group. It should be pointed out that power as the ability to perform is, as such, hard to evaluate until *it has been demonstrated* and there has been actual performance beyond the actual *ability to perform.*

It would probably be easy for most students to confuse *force* and *power* on the part of a teacher with the consequent failure to distinguish between the two. Then, too, most students do not realize the extent of their own power over their teachers. Such influence appears to be great with young teachers and to diminish gradually thereafter. Formal attempts to evaluate and report on a teacher's qualities results in publication of some type of comparative faculty rating.

Institutional colleagues oftentimes evaluate fellow teachers in terms of popularity as well as of teaching power. Administrators attempt rating teachers for placement or employment purposes as well as for salary increases, promotions, or assignments. No one can work alongside a teacher for very long without forming some kind of opinion as to how "good" he is as a teacher. One administrator said of a young teacher that "he is not much of a public speaker but in the classroom, believe me, he is a crackerjack."

Interclass visitation provides opportunities for assessing a fellow teacher's effectiveness with students on a short term basis. Such an understanding makes possible the psychological identification of members of the faculty as it is possible for some to bask in the reflected glory of others.

Employment of "big names" or "headliners" as classroom teachers is a much sought goal of some administrators. For public relations purposes, this maneuver is naturally potentially invaluable. For benefiting whole generations of students, it is extremely important. Such a move is a type of pre-evaluation of the power of a proposed new faculty member. After employment and when the performance indicates the exertion of influence of a favorable kind, then the evidence of teaching power begins to mount. Even though it takes years to assemble positive proof of the teacher's power in the lives of former students it must be conceded that such an occurrence dated back to his early attempts to influence his pupils.

Teachers of power are much sought after especially by those who perceive the work of a teacher to be agents of change. Such teachers who can and do influence pupils to a marked degree possess a quality which enables them to move to new positions almost at will. Their mobility within the profession is only a matter of exercising their choices. Teachers who have largely lost their power have practically no chances to move upward or even outward in their pursuit of new positions. This is true whether geographical changes or promotional opportunities are desired. Developing power and increasing it regularly operates as a door-opener in terms of employment opportunities and professional honors. Tardy recognition of teaching power is sometimes delayed beyond retirement or even death of the teacher. His influence and power to change his former students, however, lives on and on if he has lighted the little spark, kindled it, and encouraged it into a permanent flame which will not let the learner go. Early in the century, a researcher described the question of a powerful teacher as having "torpedo" effects. Inquiry which enters a life with an explosion which never again permits a return to the pre-question era must surely come from a powerful source. Teachers who can stir up and cause students to reconstruct their experiences in such a way as to grow, are surely entitled to an evaluation report on their obvious power to teach in a meaningful way on a permanent basis.

CRITERIA FOR EVALUATION OF POWER

Even though the yardstick is missing, there are several ways of judging teaching effectiveness which are in current usage. After satisfying the usual basic requirement of certification, employment, and health, administrative personnel rely in the main on both favorable reports and the absence of negative information. In-service ratings by superintendents, principals, supervisors, teacher educators, departmental leaders, state departmental inspectors, and co-ordinators as well as self-ratings from teachers themselves all deal with teaching effectiveness. Indirectly, school marks and achievement reports of pupils, if conscientiously awarded, reflect to a considerable degree on the teachers' effectiveness.

Some of the most used criteria for judging teaching effectiveness appear as lists of characteristics of successful teachers. Corresponding lists of qualities of poor or unsuccessful teachers are also in existence. One representative list of such traits was prepared by Cole after considerable research on the subject.[12] Beyond the immediate classroom situation, the ultimate criteria for judging teaching power is to be found in an examination of the pupils post-school achievement which can be traced to the influence of teachers. School success is important but not particularly relevant to the long-range decision on teaching power. For while almost uncontrolled teacher judgment is called into play in determining both the quality and quantity of pupil learning, similar uncontrolled opinions are developed by former pupils who gradually adjudge ihe power and influence of their teachers after years of experience with and application of the teachings. These changes which teachers patiently work in the lives of learners testify eloquently to the power of the instruction.

When one reflects upon the variables in the picture, it is no wonder that the criteria for judging teaching effectiveness are so difficult to discover. It may be impossible to assess teaching power through discovering and formulating criteria for all teachers at all times in all aspects of teaching. The only possibility may be to take one teacher, at one time, in one aspect of teaching and discover the effectiveness and so deduce or adduce the general criteria for the one case.

Teachers, in their own thinking, tend to classify themselves as neither outstandingly good nor poor but in the "average" category. The area is a no-man's land of uncertainties for there is no one generally accepted merit rating criterion for teachers. Subjectivity reigns almost supreme in the judgments of school administrators on this score. Looming large in most private formulas for rating are such general items as dependability, service, relationships, appearance, stability, and personality. The rating and the interpretation both hinge upon the subjective judgment of the rater and interpreter. In the light of such facts, the leaders of the profession of teaching are not particularly anxious to endorse such unobjective ratings especially when employment and income are keyed to the subjective interpretations. Some plans which call for teacher committee action to pass upon merit are also viewed with suspicion. The trend is definitely away from such merit ratings as those described above for their obvious weaknesses do a disservice to the teachers who deserve better treatment.

The great Ulich[13] has stated that a student should not be given mere results. Far better, he asserts, is to develop an understanding of "the principles and methods which have guided the seekers in their search toward wisdom." In a very real sense, then, the teacher who follows the latter plan would be more effective in the long run. For what profit anyone who in a teaching-learning situation learns of results but fails to acquire the skill of producing results again at will should the necessity arise? For many years, the University of Chicago has employed techniques in the measuring of learning which cover both the results and the nine important principles and methods.[14] In addition to the cognitive knowledge, other elements evaluated were:

1. Knowledge — the recall of either specific or general information which was included in various parts of the course. The information may include knowledge of terms, specific facts, trends, classifications, criteria, methods, principles and generalizations, or theories.

2. Comprehension — the ability to understand and interpret an idea, a work, or a passage. This may include the ability to translate an idea or work from one form to another as well as skill in summarizing data or documents.
3. Application — the ability to use principles, generalizations, ideas, or methods in new problem situations in order to solve the problem, tc explain a particular phenomenon, or to predict the consequences of a particular action.
4. Analysis — the ability to determine the relationship among the parts of a work or passage and to discover the organization and arrangement of the work.
5. Synthesis — the ability to integrate and organize ideas, specific evidence, and arguments to form a whole.
6. Evaluation — the ability to appraise and judge a policy, a work, or a specific viewpoint in terms of criteria. This includes the ability to evaluate one work in the light of the theory and criteria formed by another.

The important element in the University of Chicago plan for evaluation was the opportunity provided to teacher and student to overcome any noted defects without delay. The analysis of strengths and weaknesses for an individual could be the foundation for independent study and the selections of future courses, along with conferences with skilled advisers who regularly help overcome academic problems. Pooling of information in learning progress of one's students would certainly throw much information on the teacher's performance. Indeed, stripped of all rationalization, it is safe to assert that a teacher should not have credit for effective teaching unless a majority of his students has been affirmatively influenced by his teachings. Of course, even then, all the credit would not likely belong to a single teacher nor to all teachers collectively as factors inherent in students usually contribute much to good learning results.

Evidence does not support the theory that scores on teacher rating scales and pupil growth reports are related. Supervisory ratings of teachers even cannot be trusted to relate to pupil attainment. In short, teacher ratings measure one thing, while tests of pupil growth measure another. It is argued that it might be and probably would be an erroneous conclusion to credit a given teacher with all pupil growth as a result of a high score on a teacher rating scale. Similarly it would be equally faulty procedure to adjudge a given teacher to be powerful because of high achievement scores of her pupils. Power cannot be so summarily judged. The principle of multiple causation should be considered as well as pupil factors, and the necessity for time to elapse to permit the promise to be fulfilled.

No one seems to have perfected a way of predicting teaching effectiveness. There are so many variables which affect a teacher's effectiveness that an investigation concerned with predicting teaching success would be exceedingly difficult to design. The separate areas of personal relations, knowledge and use of subject matter, knowledge and use of methodology, and group management would have to be checked both before and during teaching. Current appraisals of the quality of teaching reveal much needed research of a long-term and large scale type to show by extensive investigation directions in which teacher educators should move in their progress of preparation.

On the college level, the human dimension in teaching has been neglected. Hilgard's summary is that

> "It is surprising that, after all these years of doing it, we know so very little about effective teaching."

but he believes

> "that we can study the effectiveness with which we teach, and we can continue to improve."[15]

Even on the subject of faculty work loads on the college level, the amount of knowledge we have about teachers is meager. Stechlein says:

> "Very few businessmen or institutions of comparable size, complexity, and diversity of function operate with as little knowledge and understanding of the basic activities of their workers as do most colleges and universities. Even in college where size is not a factor, little is usually known about faculty activities over and above the assigned classroom meetings with students, and a few committee assignments."[16]

Classroom observation by a supervisory specialist for the purpose of teacher effectiveness is possible at the present time but accurate measurement is not. It is not because teacher effectiveness must in the long run be determined on the basis of effects on pupils and their behavior. While the teaching and learning are in process, it would seem to be too early to assess the changes in behavior which are expected to flow from the new learnings. Indeed, no one knows at the time of teaching just how much has been learned or the quality factors either. In short, time is an essential factor in the evaluation of teaching effectiveness. Thus, assuming what was taught was learned in the ordinary sense of the term, evaluators would still have to await the day when application would affirmatively appear for not all of that which is "learned" is ever used.

The classroom attitudes of teachers of the authoritarian types and the non-authoritarian types do not reveal differences in basic teaching power.[17]

An observer, following the assignments and activities of the school, might well analyze the types of experiences the learners are having. Dale, in his famous "Cone of Experience" shows those believed to reflect greater value to students at the base of the cone with others less valuable ascending the ladder. In trying to determine which experiences are potentially more beneficial to pupils, Dale concludes that direct, purposeful experiences rate at the top.

His famous "Cone of Experience" shows clearly the progression from direct purposeful experience to more complex abstractions.[18] Applied to teaching, it is evident that teaching power is involved in the choices and provision for the several categories of learning experiences. Ordinarily, in terms of expected degrees of teaching power, the "cone" would fit from the base upwards. Unfortunately, much instruction is conducted on the reverse order either of necessity or by choice.

What are the powers of the teacher? Beyond the areas of rights, obligations, responsibilities, relationships, duties, privileges, and *authority,* teachers have exercised power from time immemorial, and they will continue to do so. Among these super-power might be identified with those positive and negative illustrations:

(Positive) a. Lasting influence through help in "doing" rather than just "hearing."

(Negative) b. Lifetime dislike for whole areas — reverse motivation — learning plateau.

By observing the "Laws of Learning"[19] an instructor is, ordinarily, able to improve his teaching effectiveness. But let it be clearly understood, the "Laws of Learning" are not artificially contrived formulas for good teaching. They are at best the summations of how learning occurred under given circumstances as observed by Thorndike and others around the turn of the century and since that time. They are natural but not normative, and they cannot be "broken" or "disobeyed" as a rule enjoined or a legal prescription demanding conformation.

ANALYSIS OF TEACHING POWER AND STYLE

Teaching power is another way of indicating instructional effectiveness. Among the factors related to and in most cases contributing to a teacher's power are the following:

1. The particular style employed.
   (This includes methodology)
2. Knowledge of and ability to "prepare" subject matter for use.
   Where it is and organization for teaching-learning
3. Ability to manage, discipline, and control a group of learners
   (This includes motivation of individuals)
4. Ability to communicate from a basis of experiential knowledge.
   (This includes making oneself heard and understood)
5. Personality, poise, and fairness in classroom situations.
   (This includes development of respect of students)
6. Knowing exactly the destination and taking a direct route to it.
7. An understanding of the general nature of learners with special recognition for their individual problems.
8. An understanding of the so-called "Laws of Learning" and how they were derived.

Indeed, in a strict juristic or moral sense, there are no true laws of learning which, if observed, will guarantee or insure increased teaching power. Reliance upon historical rules, or substitution of the more modern "gadget approach" to instruction are both likely to lead to unproductive results in the long run. There is a very real foundation for the concept that the public has every right to specify "what" shall be taught in schools, but that the "how" should be left to the teachers themselves. Doubtless the underlying reason for this observation is that to obtain maximum personal teaching power, the style should be selected by the user on the basis of diverse considerations, not the least of which might well be the personal desires, strengths, defects, and limitations of the instructor. Indeed such "laws" may very well be changed at least in emphasis over a period of time. For the present they should, from the individual teacher or pupil's point of view, remain indicative and explanatory, not imperative, not admonitory.

As students of history have observed, teaching skill and power would appear to be relative to time, place, personnel, discipline, and most of all to the increasing knowledge about the complicated teaching-learning process itself. For what was at one time, one place, by certain personnel, in a given discipline, with the current status of knowledge of the teaching-learning process, considered to be an excellent performance, we now might consider it very poor indeed. Such drastic evaluatory swings has led one philosopher-statesman to observe that what was once an evil is now by common practice and consent considered a virtue, and what was once a virtue is with some disgust branded a "sin." The much besmirched lecture was once one of the finest teaching practices. But that was in the day when reading materials were much less plentiful than they are today. With great logic, it has been argued that it has outlived its usefulness and now largely contributes to slothfulness and a form of mis-education.

Not much change of substance can be found from an examination of two generations of both teacher and student thinking and writing about teacher effectiveness. The problem of rating teaching power remains virtually unresolved with all its attendant issues. The periodical literature on the subject from the late

Twenties on down to the middle Sixties only reveals more sophistication in the positions taken, more experience in the stating of the dimensions of the broad concepts related to the problem, and a continued interest in making some progress. Throughout the 35 year period, major emphasis was placed on descriptive, administrative and methodological approaches. Analytical attacks appeared to be limited to the devices for rating teachers. The literature reflects a wide range of attempts to shed light on what was even before 1930, an apparent professional headache. Among the various articles may be found such categories as the following: estimations of efficiency; appraisals of teaching; assessment of teaching ability; and measuring of teaching success. Among the devices written about before 1930 were the score cards, observation record forms, check lists, and rating scales. Scattered articles appeared on such subjects as testing, personal traits, promotions, methods, administration, and problems of rating teachers.

There has been relatively stable production of articles on the subject of teacher rating for over thirty years with the exception of the war years when the number of such articles apparently slackened. In the late Fifties an increase in publication of teacher rating articles was noted. Since 1961, however, fewer indexed articles have been published on this professional problem.

There seems to have been much more emphasis on pay, promotions, and tenure in the literature of the Sixties. Such considerations were described as the cases for and against merit pay with "Keys" to merit rating, evaluation as the key to tenure, along with the psychological and historical approaches to teacher evaluation.

Following along the same general trend has been the production of articles on student rating of teachers. Student demands, expectations, and attitudes toward teachers are all chronicled in the later literature. Pupil imagery of teachers, their reactions to them, and their memories of favorites are interestingly set forth. Stress appears to be given to what pupils like, what they think, and what they do as reflecting the effectiveness of the teaching they are receiving. But no one has discovered the secret of rating teacher effectiveness; nobody has the answer to the most persistent challenge of society to education's longest running controversy.

In the history of American education, "facts" are elusive. One can never be sure that the final answer has been given in regard to matters past, present, or future. In fact, it is almost certain that so many changes will occur that all one can believe is that there is nothing but transition. This is a constant challenge to students who are interested in research but who recognize that "fact" in one sense is related rather closely to the circumstances of time and place. Beliefs, however, are warranted in the light of the records we have preserved and the logical inferences which we may derive from them, providing our conclusions are consistent with the present forms of education which most certainly have grown out of the past. No student of the history of American education can study long without concluding that this enterprise has always had a bright, glowing, even promising future, and about all that can be said with certainty now is that American education is a "becoming" institution. When and where it will arrive, is anyone's guess. Before it does arrive at professional maturity, the challenge of society to recognize excellence in teaching in tangible as well as intangible considerations is indicated.

Chapter 4

Accentuation of Teaching Power

It is difficult to imagine a teaching-learning situation in which there was not room for improvement. Though we are scarcely conscious of the fact, the ordinary experience of each of us probably offers ample evidence of this situation. In one sense, if evaluation of teaching power could be made at a certain point in time, recognition that the zenith had not been reached would surely be obvious. When one considers the vast reservoir of potential subject-matter coupled with literally dozens of possibilities for presentation to pupils who in turn have their own peculiar learning problems and individual differences, it is no wonder that there is a margin for enhancing the influence of the teacher. This chapter deals with suggestions for doing just that.

Interwoven with the direct dealings between a teacher and his pupils are the inclinations and needs of both as the inclinations suggest and the needs compel, myriads of antecedents lead to practices universally deemed customary in the teacher-pupil relationship. To enhance teaching power, it is often necessary to break into acknowledged practices which have acquired respectability over the years. Through adaptations, innovation, experimentation, research, and eternal vigilance, progress can usually be made. This is particularly true wherever there is a marriage of intense desire and trial applications of intuitive leanings. Standard practices and procedures yield to conscientious attempts to employ findings obtained through feedback, action research, getting to know students better, rejection of unethical approaches, team contributions, programing, and scientific evaluation.

Highly motivated able and ambitious young people come to schools and colleges not to be given anything, but rather to get something. That something is, in the main, an organized opportunity for self-education which undoubtedly exists at each of the thousands of schools and colleges in this country. Just as some of these institutions are, in terms of size, wealth, age, or costs, higher than others, so also, some of the students are higher in their motivation, ability, and ambition to get an education. Shared in common, however, is the individual vision of greatness through personal accomplishments based on knowledge of greatness of the institution and its distinguished alumni.

It really isn't so much what the university or school has done or can do to provide teaching power to students as that happy combination of determination for self-development on the learner's part along with the physical plant, ample study materials, and a faculty also with the qualities of high motivation, ability and ambition to serve as examples for the learners. This environment, dynamic and electrifying, is most favorable to intellectual, social, and other types of rapid value growth. Parents cannot measure in terms of dollars, the great benefits such an environment can help produce. Their main responsibility is met admirably when, after due inquiry, and careful investigation of relevant factors, an institution is selected that will do what needs to be done. Of course, most American sons and daughters could find not one but several schools, colleges, and universities which would be considered "right" for them from the viewpoints of educational counselors.

Potential students are so different in their personalities, social and academic backgrounds, health, and other characteristics that very few specific guides to their future learning experiences can be made. An example is provided in the way the Harvard Law School Handbook for entering students treats of notetaking which is obviously very important and highly recommended to all, without, however, being dogmatically specific on "how" to accomplish the task.

> Successful classroom work is a combination of thinking, discussion and note-taking.
>
> There are as many ways to take notes as there are students. You will see all possible techniques. Most peculiar are the Independent Thinkers, those people who don't take notes

in class and spend most of their time "mulling over" the law. Next are the Key Idea Jotters, those who jot down only the essence of a case or the most felicitous bon mot of the professor.

Then there are the Treatise Writers who make rough outlines of the cases, class notes, and law review articles which are later combined into one magnum opus, usually typed. You may also see Encyclopaedists, the chaps with the many colors of ink who take lecture notes in black, abstract the cases in red, summarize law review articles in green, distill their own observations in purple — all this on the same page of their notebooks, in the margins and between the lines. The Stenos are the ones with the weird combination of Gregg shorthand, cryptic abbreviations and untiring penmanship who take down everything said in class down to the "Ahem" of the professor.

The amazing thing is that there seems to be little relation between the technique of note-taking and success. Each of you has limitations and abilities which will pretty much determine how you will take notes. Those gifted with a retentive memory can be brief. The rapid writers can be more complete. Most of you who are neither will have to find a middle ground by trial and error during the first few weeks.

A few guiding hints:

DON'T try to be a stenographer if it prevents you from thinking about what is going on in class.

DON'T try to be too selective at first, you cannot be sure what is relevant and what is not.

DON'T ignore what your fellow students have to say, it often is valuable.

DON'T miss taking down the questions your professor poses, even at the expense of not hearing the answer. The questions are the things he has given thought to, the answers are often off-the-cuff or tentative.[1]

All schools, but particularly colleges and universities, are charged in our society with the responsibilities of transmitting the cultural heritage in an enriched form, developing the talents of all of our people, and in developing new knowledge. Regardless of the labels or forms of announced objectives, purposes, aims, goals, whether temporary or ultimate in classification, the meaning and mission of education are subject to institutional adjustment and interpretation. This is necessary in our civilization to insure the liberty with which our educational leaders can build strong bulwarks of freedom in our country.

Even as the church mothered the schools, so the schools have, through their contributions to our way of life, greatly assisted in the struggle for intellectual, political, economic and social emancipation for the American people over the centuries.

Every institution of education has objectives. Some are hard to find in a formal type of statement; others have more than one set of aims. Most schools have changed their purposes from the time of their establishment to the present. If a realistic analysis were made of the changing purposes of a given university, no doubt there would be some type of general pronouncement, concerning the whole institution for all of its history. Along with such a broad, historical or descriptive statement, there would very likely be understood objectives for each division of the university. And then, on further looking one would find objectives for departments or sections, for curricula, and for each of the courses and even units, lessons, or parts of lessons.

As individual teachers, faculties and the profession at large, we should do everything within our power to improve our teaching power. Not that we need to apologize now for what we have accomplished, but the problem of improving teaching in terms of both quality and quantity is, perhaps, the major educational challenge of our generation and perhaps the entire century. On its resolution hinges the future welfare of millions of people. And, if one is to believe what he hears and reads, the quality of teaching and learning in many American schools leaves much to be desired. A diagnosis of the quality of education based on several years of study shows that it falls short of what it could be.[2]

It is time for consideration of the important question of "Who guards the guardians of knowledge?" If the answer is "the school superintendents, boards, trustees, regents, curators, and parents of the students," then we must ask if any or all of these "guardians" are able to identify powerful teaching. If so, have they rewarded it suitably with the coin of the realm? Have they taken a realistic look at the quality of education provided for their own community, analyzed it thoroughly from every angle, communicated the facts to all interested, and taken steps for future progress?

When one gets right down to the truth, very few people can change very much. This theory might be called predestination, or environmental causation, or whatever you will, but the fact remains: outside of physical development, the individual human being's real changes are few and very slowly acquired. However true this may be, teaching is predicated on the possibility of change — or perhaps more accurately stated, on the theory that guided growth is the better part of wisdom. There is current a theory which is supported by a school of counselors to the effect that "You can't teach anybody to teach anything."[3] In terms of motivity, desire to learn, effort and application, it is recognized that the major burden falls upon the learner himself.

The student who "learns," or merely becomes familiar with subject matter of a course but declines to apply or use what he has learned, that is, he takes a "so what" attitude, demonstrates an academic sickness and needs help. This thing of going through the motion of learning but in truth and in fact not even wanting to learn is an abomination to the teaching profession. Drastic therapy is indicated if constant self-examination and acquisition of new knowledge do not lead to changes and heightened activity for improvements. Intellectual hyprocrisy posing as scholarliness is not limited to students but may extend to teachers as well.

The teaching profession has, among other purposes, an unending goal: the improvement of teaching power and all that this comprises. Even if we suffer each teacher to teach as he thinks fit and give freedom of instruction so that he is free to apply his own theories and follow his own bent, the problem of improving teaching power looms large in our time. For the growth of knowledge which in former times was slow and even slight, has now become rapid and great. Space exploration alone has opened up an entirely new frontier with grave implications for the leaders in education. And the problems of education appear to be increasing in complexity as rapid advances in technology are announced. Careful observers of the educational scene tend to believe that it is a herculean task just to keep pace with the never-ending parade let alone make gains.

The key to teaching power is to be found in the relationship which develops between the teacher and the taught. For most education is really a matter of personal stimulation which one person exerts upon another through personal contacts. Bell has aptly put the situation:

> A conference is always better than a lecture because in the latter one person does all the work while in the former at least two persons interact upon one another. Almost any thoughtful man or woman who has been through college will testify that the chief sources of profit to him or her in that experience came not from courses of study, from facts accumulated, from books read or experiments performed, but rather from intelligent and stimulating persons met.[4]

A wise observer has well summed up the goal of American education and of teachers:

> American education has set for itself the goal of developing free men. That is to say, its major purpose is to train people who are able to think for themselves, exercise judgment and act upon that judgment, and deeply care...
> ...chief purpose is to call men to think for themselves.[5]

Those who have "finished" their schooling can never forget that education is not achieved by time serving, having a good time, or going through the empty motions of studying and learning. On looking back, it is evident that our "education" was surely a process of "becoming" wherein an individual's problems were attacked with vigor. Those who confuse their expectations in going to school sometimes pretend that course work calls for memorizing and reciting answers to asked or unasked questions. Overcoming the hurdles of a course seems to be an end in itself. It is true that basic information courses are necessary as a means to an end. With reference to methodological possibilities, Garrison in *The Adventures of Learning in College,* says

Less obvious, but often as important, is the kind of class, where you may witness a skilled teacher attack a problem, analyze it, and solve it (within limits he proposes) in a way that could instruct you or cause you to want to imitate him. For example, a brilliant lecturer will give you the chance to see and appreciate a distinctive competence and a distinctive commitment to a particular intellectual understanding.[6]

This process of "becoming" definitely calls for the person who espouses the role of the scholar to think critically, develop his vocabulary, engage in simple research, motivate himself, communicate correctly and effectively, develop satisfactory personal relationships, engage in various independent study projects, discipline himself, challenge himself, all to the end that he attacks his own problems and follows through to their resolution. In this connection, the "role" includes special attention to health and well-being in the various areas generally designated as the physical, social, mental, and spiritual. Attention to "wholeness" or "soundness" or "the golden mean" pay dividends to the ambitious student.

The wise student knows that if he gets an education, he is going to have to get it himself. It cannot be given to him. It is not to be confused with its popular substitutes as so often is the case among the uninitiated.

ENHANCING TEACHING POWER THROUGH OBJECTIVES

The chief cause of poor teaching is aimlessness. This, obviously, is not confined to the teacher but characteristically extends to at least some of the students in a given class. A clearly conceived aim appears to control a given school course and some courses unfortunately claim to have as many as a dozen or more.

In the first place, there are various terms which denote the objective of either the teacher or the students. Used synonymously with the term "objective" are these: goals, aims, desired ends, purposes. Then as a refinement of the concept, there are long-term versus short-term objectives, ultimate versus present, general versus specific, permanent versus temporary, long range, intermediate and immediate aims. These objectives are not to be invented by the teacher but discovered as already existing.

Objectives are to be formulated by the teacher, sometimes with the help of the pupils, after a very careful study of the needs of the pupils has been made. After discovery of pupil needs and problems has been made, a decision is made as to what shall be the object of the prolonged effort of the teacher and the members of the class. The formal statement of what is desired to be accomplished constitutes the objective. Discussing the origin of objectives, Tyler has stated

> "...no single source of information is adequate to provide a basis for wise and comprehensive decisions about objectives of the school"[7]

In turning to the source of educational objectives he has specifically recommended studies of learners themselves, of life outside the school, suggestions from subject specialists, and the uses of both philosophy and psychology.

The powerful teacher has a way of encouraging students to formulate their own personal learning objectives. This self-discovery leads to many benefits in the long run. Even if a teacher should formulate a statement of learning objectives, he would take great pains to have them understood and accepted by each learner, otherwise much effort would be wasted on the part of the students who were not really oriented and working with the teacher. The maximum use of objectives can be obtained by using them in the selection and making of assignments, the conduct of class recitations and discussions, and by no means least, in the preparation and interpretation of the tests and examinations. Teachers without vision fail to see the possibilities of objectives throughout the entire process of teaching, oftentimes stopping their use in the initial stage of assignment making. Not so, the powerful teacher who relies heavily on objectives as the guide lines for the entire professional task of guiding the developmental learning tasks of pupils.

The powerful teacher understands that objectives enter into the selection of appropriate methods of teaching. Indeed, the astute teacher quickly learns that the objective practically dictates the choice of teaching procedure which is calculated to bring the most effective results. And this method which was made a part of the learning process and fully in line with the objective being achieved, extends itself far beyond the given class or even year in which the learning was performed. Sometimes, and hopefully, it will stand the learner in good stead for the remainder of his life, producing benefits over and over again for him.

One of the finest advances made in the formulation and use of teaching objectives was pioneered by Watkins. He has given us a list of the standards by which objectives may be judged in an attempt to decide whether they are acceptable or not. The powerful teacher makes every attempt to start with good objectives, knowing that faulty aims will detract from the teacher's effectiveness to help his pupils. The criteria for judging objectives as listed by Watkins follow:

Suggested Criteria for Judging
Course or Unit Objectives[8]

1. Can pupils interpret the objectives for themselves?
2. Does each objective fit the course or unit for which it is stated better than it fits any other course or unit?
3. Does each objective indicate some value other than an appeal to general discipline?
4. Can each objective be reached within reasonable time limits?
5. Does each objective indicate some definite value other than preparation for later school work?
6. Is each objective consistent with the intrinsic function of the subject matter?
7. Are objectives stated in terms of the effect upon the learner?

He might well have added an eighth:

Is each objective consistent with the other objectives of the school?

ENHANCING TEACHING POWER THROUGH PRINCIPLES

The powerful teacher does not "give" his pupils "knowledge" but rather teaches them how to develop it for themselves. As such, teaching is a venture in faith and a labor of love. It is not an exercise in superficial imitation nor is it composed of myriad activities which on the surface appear to be within the capability of anyone regardless of his personal attributes and qualities. For teaching to be powerful calls for a certain type of leadership which we might describe as dynamic in that it is a change agent with versatility, high purpose, and boundless energy.

The powerful teacher is called upon to live by principles of teaching which really produce effective results. Butler, in a treatise which has given American teachers new perspective for over 25 years, has listed the following principles which have been tested and found valuable by those who wish to improve their teaching.[9]

Principle 1: The objectives should be most worthwhile.

Principle 2: Pupils learn through self-activity, but this activity should be psychologically sound.

Principle 3: Self-activity to be psychologically sound should be in fullest agreement with the type or types of learning involved in attaining the objectives.

Principle 4: Learning should be unitary, not fragmentary.

Principle 5: The energy of pupils should be released so that they apply themselves fully.

Principle 6: Teaching should provide for individual differences.

Principle 7: Teaching should be diagnostic and remedial.

Principle 8: The physical and social environment for learning should be ideal.

ENHANCING TEACHING POWER THROUGH STANDARDS

The finest set of standards which has incidentally gained national recognition since it was formulated at mid-century, is known as the California Statement of Teaching Competence. It was developed under the auspices of the Teacher Education and Professional Standards Commission of the National Education Association of the United States. Many a teacher, wishing to improve his over-all effectiveness, has had favorable results from studying this document and developing strengths in what appeared to be his weak areas of performance. It should be pointed out that the Statement is the result of cooperative action by a wide segment of the teaching profession and that it has stood the test of time and application by teachers themselves. The Statement, while long, is an excellent instrument for use either with one, a few, or many teachers in their efforts to improve. It has also been of value to supervisors and administrators who wished to study possible areas of in-service training before making recommendations or arrangements for such further education.

CALIFORNIA STATEMENT OF TEACHING COMPETENCE

A. *The competent teacher provides for the learning of students.*

1. Uses psychological principles of learning.
    - (a) Uses effective and continuing motivation.
    - (b) Organizes varied learning activities to meet student interests and needs.
    - (c) Directs learning activities according to a sequential, developmental pattern.
2. Uses principles of child growth and development in learning situations.
    - (a) Provides differentiated activities and assignments to meet the needs and abilities of students.
    - (b) Knows the health (mental and physical) status of students and adapts activities to their needs.
3. Maintains an atmosphere in the classroom that is conducive to learning and is marked by a sense of balance between freedom and security.
    - (a) Maintains an effective working situation.
    - (b) Provides opportunities for students to cooperate and to exercise leadership in the activities of large and small groups.

(c) Provides opportunity for expression of independent critical thought with emphasis on freedom of expression and openmindedness.

4. Plans effectively.
   (a) Aids the students to define worthwhile objectives for large units, daily class work, and special class activities.
   (b) Organizes his teaching well by choosing wisely learning experiences, subject matter content, and materials of instruction.

5. Uses varied teaching procedures.
   (a) Uses teaching procedures (such as group reporting, discussion, planning with pupils) designed to achieve desired purposes in teaching.
   (b) Builds effectively upon the students' participation in class activities.
   (c) Develops study skills of students.
   (d) Stimulates creative activities of students.
   (e) Aids the students to evaluate their own achievements.

6. Uses diagnostic and remedial procedures effectively.
   (a) Is familiar with common diagnostic tests in his own and related fields.
   (b) Constructs, administers, and interprets diagnostic tests.
   (c) Uses other appropriate diagnostic procedures.

7. Uses adequate procedures for evaluating the achievement of students.
   (a) Uses informal evaluation procedures (anecdotal record, interview, questionnaire) for collecting and interpreting needed information.
   (b) Uses standard achievement tests.
   (c) Uses teacher-made tests.
   (d) Keeps accurate and adequate records, e.g., case studies, cumulative records.
   (e) Makes effective reports to students and parents concerning the progress of students in their growth.

8. Manages the class effectively.
    (a) Plans satisfactory routine for the handling of materials, equipment, and supplies.
    (b) Uses own and pupils' time effectively.
    (c) Is attentive to the physical well-being of students in such matters as heating, lighting, ventilation, and seating.

B. *The competent teacher counsels and guides students wisely.*

1. Uses sound psychological principles concerning the growth and development of children in guiding individuals and groups.
    (a) Maintains objectivity when dealing with behavior that is aggressive and abnormal.
    (b) Is sympathetic with and sensitive to students' personal and social problems as well as their academic needs.
    (c) Makes adjustments in the curriculum and other requirements in light of pupils' needs.
    (d) Secures sufficient rapport with students so that they come voluntarily for counsel.
    (e) Collects and uses significant counseling data as aptitude and intelligence test results.
    (f) Uses suitable counseling procedures.
2. Maintains effective relationships with parents.
    (a) Explains the needs, abilities, interests, and problems of the students to their parents.
    (b) Obtains cooperation from parents in helping students with their problems.

C. *The competent teacher aids students to understand and appreciate our cultural heritage.*

1. Organizes the classroom for effective democratic living.
2. Directs individuals and groups to significant life applications of classroom learnings.
    (a) Uses subject fields to develop understanding of social, economic, and political problems.

(b) Develops an understanding of the wide significance of various fields of subject matter.

3. Draws on his own background of experiences to elicit the cultural growth of individuals and groups.

4. Helps students to know and to apply in their daily lives the democratic principles which are rooted deep in our historical development.

D. *The competent teacher participates effectively in the activities of the school.*

1. Plans cooperatively the means of achieving educational objectives.
   (a) Shares effectively in curriculum revision and is able to evaluate progress toward attaining educational objectives.
   (b) Shows flexibility in modifying his plans and procedures to fit with those of the entire school.

2. Assumes his share of the responsibility for school activities.
   (a) Carries out effectively the administrative responsibilities delegated to him.
   (b) Participates in planning and administering extracurricular activities.
   (c) Maintains harmonious personal relations with his colleagues.

E. *The competent teacher assists in maintaining good relations between the school and the rest of the community.*

1. Acquaints himself with available community resources and uses them in classroom activities.

2. Obtains the cooperation of parents in school activities.

3. Aids in defining and solving community problems.

4. Takes part in community affairs and projects.

5. Observes professional ethics in discussing school problems particularly with lay persons.

F. *The competent teacher works on a professional level.*

1. Gives evidence of the social importance of the profession to parents, students, and other members of the profession.
2. Adheres to a professional code of ethics.
3. Contributes to the profession by membership in professional organizations and participation in their activities.
4. Assumes responsibility for his own professional growth by planning an appropriate program for professional betterment.
5. Aids in supervising student teachers and in the orientation and induction of beginning teachers.[10]

ENHANCING TEACHING THROUGH EXPERIMENTATION AND RESEARCH

In a delightful small book, Stephen Corey has outlined multiple opportunities for teachers to become more effective through what he describes as "action research."[11] The teacher who wishes to develop more power in teaching should engage in experimentation and research continuously. In one sense of the term, this is what teaching *is* and what it always will be. For school and the classroom are problem solving places — places where a problem or problems may be attacked vigorously not only by the one with the problem but with a helper or helpers besides. Problems which do not yield to this type of action will ordinarily yield when subject-matter consultants or specialists in such problems are obtained. The most obvious reason why a person goes to school is to have his needs met and his problems solved. Sometimes when neither the pupil nor the teacher is very alert, the school year can start and end without substantial progress made on a given problem. Sometimes, too, the real problems are ignored and artificial or imagined ones are dealt with. This is not the case with a powerful teacher who uses intelligence in diagnosing the situation, knowledge and experience in finding the means to a solution, courage in applying the corrective, and strength to carry the remedy on to its final triumph. In more ways than one, teaching is a "do it yourself" enterprise from the teacher's point of view, when, as it sometimes seems, those closest to the problem or need, fail to see or understand it, neglect to attack it directly, yet while oblivious to it, expect the teacher to produce miracles. Just as the scientific process of solving problems calls for patience and skill, so, too, does teaching. Really before much progress can be made in overcoming needs and problems of learners, the process of research and experimentation will have to be instigated and results known. Then as the instruction proceeds, so too will research and experimentation accompany the powerful teacher's efforts to substantially influence the learner for the balance of his life. The whole purpose of follow-up studies would appear to be an effort to find out whether the teachers' power has been extended beyond the classroom into the life after school. Some teachers in their modesty believe that former pupils, now with more maturity, will be more cognizant of the school's influences. What was disliked vehemently in school, sometimes years later is reported by former students to be valuable. This is one form of experimentation and research which, while too late for those who are reporting, is still of some value to those still in school and it also finds a place in the evaluation of a teacher's former and still current effectiveness with former pupils.

ENHANCING TEACHING POWER THROUGH ADAPTATIONS AND INNOVATIONS

The best of teachers have to innovate and adapt. Those who aim to be of maximum service to their pupils are sensitive to the information available when pupils react to the teacher, assignments, learning activities, and evaluative situations. This has been described as "feedback" and can be extremely valuable to a teacher in his attempts to adapt the requirements to the needs and problems of learners.

Devices which illustrate the feedback principle are thermostats on home heating and air conditioning plants, the governor on gasoline engines, a radio which, hooked to a clock, turns itself on and off on schedule, the elevator's mechanism which prevents a door from opening when the elevator is between floors, electric eye to open doors, turn lights on and off, and a record player which turns itself off. While these are mechanically regulated, teachers have to read the signs mostly from non-verbal communications and translate these into changed assignments, attempts to help promptly with problem situations, and the usual responses to calls for help on the part of students. A frown on the face of a pupil during a teacher explanation could be interpreted as a failure to understand which might be responded to by a re-explanation, or by the giving of different examples or illustrations until the light dawned. The teacher to be effective should control the learning situation on the basis of actual performance rather than on what was originally expected. To continue in an original plan while observing that something has gone wrong is not the mark of a powerful teacher. Clearly in this situation, adaptations and innovations are in order so that the original objective may be achieved even though the pre-planned means to the goal have had to be exchanged for other media. For knowledge of results at successive stages of the teaching process suggests instant deviations, corrections, and controls for greater efficiency. By reason of the lateness of the computations, such symbols and indices as grades, school marks, final tests and examinations, teacher opinion and all they stand for are rather poor as feedback. It is clearly too late for the teacher to change much and there is no opportunity for the student to shift even if there was an incentive of some kind still remaining in the situation. An accurate feedback on the nature of performance and accomplishment is needed during the teaching process so that the teacher and pupils will have a reasonable chance to make the adjustments and re-check the interactions for increased success in the original mission.

It is well known by successful teachers that a major inhibitor of learning is the fear on the part of the learner of exposing himself, that is, of opening himself up to the possibility of change. It does little good for a teacher to threaten, ridicule, or otherwise try to force a pupil along these lines. Power by its very nature is potential while force is applied at the moment. The teacher who would become powerful in the influencing of his pupils would certainly do well to avoid force and strive for recognition of the encumbering factors in the lives of learners before adapting instruction to his real needs and problems, one and perhaps the greatest of which is this pejorative quality inherent in the learner's personality.

Much learning is cognitive and does not immediately reflect itself in the general behavior of the person. While this may be considered merely a question of transfer, it certainly is of great consequence to the teacher who is determined to be influential in his student's future. Even if it is assumed that school life is quite unrealistic as compared with what lies ahead, or that school instruction is really a simplified version of what may eventually overtake the learner, teacher attempts to make the teaching-learning process approximate the real thing, full of surprising developments, vital and meaningful now, will all pay rich dividends. This comes through constant adaptation and innovation in the classroom, extending the learning process throughout the season and life itself, and through intelligent variation of procedures to fit the climate of the group and its members.

ENHANCING TEACHER POWER THROUGH MERIT PAY PLANS

It is hard for some people to see how increasing the pay of a teacher who is truly dedicated and conscientious in his endeavors would have any effect on his teaching power. However, on this topic it might be well to speculate on the reasonable requirements of a professional teacher in the mundane sphere so that his time and attention could be given undividedly to his calling. Otherwise, a potentially powerful teacher would not become so because of the distractions, basic demands on his time and attention, and the necessity to acquire additional income from other sources or the embarrassing situation of not being able to make ends meet thereby lowering his self-esteem and the confidence reposed in him by members of his immediate family and community leaders.

Then, too, in this country it is not only a mark of our economic system to reward the producers according to the merit and output, but a "law" of social and economic justice to see that those who greatly benefit society receive the esteem and rewards from their fellows as their just deserts.

Merit pay, for the purpose of salary differentiation, is decided on the basis of somewhat subjective qualitative judgment of a teacher's competence and performance. It may not be the only equitable way to recognize and reward teaching power, but it is one way. To date, however, attempts have been exercises in frustration for many as they tried to describe what to them seemed to be indefinable. Just because no yardsticks have been devised for measuring such effectiveness is not cause to mourn or to despair. Most school people would admit that some teachers are better than others — and that most people know who they are! Certainly pupils can sense the difference, parents realize it, administrators know it, and even the teachers themselves who are superior know it. It seems that recognition of this fact of life by matching the tangible rewards will most certainly come in time when an equitable pattern of distributing the merit pay can be discovered or developed.

The plain fact of the situation is that powerful teachers who receive inadequate salaries are substantially subsidizing the education of students. Far more alarming than this, the same families who send their children to school to be educated may be enjoying all manner of luxuries in their homes which dedicated and highly skilled teachers cannot afford. Such a situation is detrimental to the continued offering of quality education. Unless corrected with some scheme of merit pay for the top teachers, it would seem that such top teachers would be forced, through starvation for the very things parents and students enjoy, to change occupations. The flight from teaching is going on to the alarm of many. There have been suggestions that some of the most powerful teachers or potential teachers should be brought back to teaching even if society had to draft them. A far better plan would be to entice them to enter willingly and to stay once they are there by a fair plan of remuneration — call it merit pay if you wish. Society and all parts of it will suffer if education declines. On the other hand, society and all parts of it will flourish if more effective education is available and received. Merit pay would have the effect of substantially increasing efforts to prove teaching effectiveness if for nothing more than enjoying the economic rewards associated with such proof. We have powerful teachers now. To fail to reward them suitably with economic buying power is but to rob them of their rightful due. The intangible rewards are theirs, it is true, but these are not enough in our competitive society. Talent and power inevitably tend to move toward where the money is.

Too long, America has been concerned with number rather than caliber in our education. While we shall remain the champion of educating the masses, it would seem that the time has come to carry out the old saying of John Dewey when he called for better quality. For in his words, "What the best and wisest parent wants for his own child that must the community want for all its children."[12]

It would certainly seem that down through the generations, the peoples of the world have through their wisest and best leaders, wanted the best and most powerful teachers they could afford for their children.

The concept of merit pay is disturbing and repugnant to some Americans. Would a merit pay plan lead to great divisions within the ranks of the teaching profession? No one knows. But we do know that in terms of learning quantity and quality, teachers have long selected the students who are deserving and paid them with the coin of the realm — school marks, or grades, promotions, exemptions, and other marks of favor. This is regarded as only telling the truth about what has actually taken place over a period of time and is within the province of the appointed teacher to carry out. While it is certainly not an easy task, it is done and with apparent satisfaction to both students and parents. Could not a similar plan be worked out for teachers?

The merit pay plan to recognize and reward powerful teaching is either going to come in due time or teaching will suffer the untimely fate of never reaching the status of a true profession with honors, esteem, confidence and rewards enjoyed by its top flight practitioners.

ENHANCING TEACHING POWER THROUGH TENURE FOR TEACHERS

Perhaps the basic reason for granting legal tenure to teachers is the desire to enhance their teaching power. So far as a teacher is concerned, or his students, his actual tenure may be a factor in his power to teach. If it is granted that "Beginners, regardless of their degree, are not worth their salt as teachers until they have survived an on-the-job apprenticeship,"[13] then it would seem that tenure is necessary not only to prove oneself as a teacher but also, insofar as the probation period is concerned, to weed out the incompetent and unfit. In all of the discussions relating to tenure, basic to the length of service a teacher stays in one job, is the merit of the instruction. Presumably, only the meritorious are retained and given legal tenure or the non-legal or true tenure type of retention because of teaching effectiveness. Either form of tenure, then, is and should be a reflection of teaching power or at least potential teaching effectiveness with the acquisition of experience and in-service education.

ENHANCING TEACHING POWER THROUGH TEACHER LEARNING

Teaching is a many-sided process which calls for the complete dedication of the professional practitioner. Once initiated to the profession, teachers are forced by the circumstances of their responsibilities to forever learn. For truly, as has been said of old, "He who would teach must never cease to learn." This indicates what has been referred to as "In-Service Education" to distinguish it from pre-service preparation for teaching. One of the finest statements describing the work of the teacher by phases was written by Jack V. Edling and is well worth reviewing in connection with in-service training of teachers.

1. The individual and collective needs of those to be taught must be assessed continuously.
2. In order to attain the objectives of education, there must be continuing preparation of instructional materials (stimuli) to which learners may respond.
3. Learners must be exposed to instructional stimuli in ways which optimize desirable learning.
4. The behavior (responses) of learners must be evaluated constantly for adequacy and appropriateness.
5. Inadequate and inappropriate learner behavior existing after instruction and evaluation must be modified by learning experiences which are unique for the individual.

6. Records must be maintained and reports rendered at periodic intervals.[14]

To be good in one phase and poor in another is to admit ineffectiveness as a teacher. A careful analysis of the six points will prove that only one — the third — concerns itself with presentation of learning materials to the learners, while the others either prepare the teacher for this task or concern themselves with a follow-up to it. Here, then, is a wonderful opportunity for a teacher to enhance his teaching power by improving in the area or areas in which he is weak. And it goes without saying that help for the teacher is usually available within the building where he teaches. A call for help with one or more of the facets of teaching described above might be directed to the principal, a fellow teacher, a supervisor, or in some cases to the students themselves who probably would welcome such an invitation to concern themselves with the needs of the teacher. This might strengthen the relationship which forms the basis of the real quality of teacher effectiveness.

Now clearly, a teacher who assigns students to use the library should be a library fan himself. Not only does a powerful teacher teach by precept but by example also. The old adage of "Do as I tell you, not as I do" has not appealed to better teachers, nor for that matter to the good leaders in any endeavor. Actions do speak louder than words with many people and the teacher who provides the example of "ever learning" will be a powerful incentive to pupils to do the same. Carrying on a course of independent study which supplements and complements the formal line of instruction is a characteristic of the most influential teachers. One need not go so far as to observe that publication and writing accompany the teachers who distinguish themselves, but it is true that an inquiring mind and scholarly endeavors are marks of greatness in the teaching profession.

One of the ideas that has continued to intrigue educators is the obvious belief that teachers need to return periodically for renewed facts of education with which to "keep up to date" on. Even while in school, there has been a growing concern with education beyond the facts, that is to say, the implications and applications of generalizations flowing from and based on the specifics of given situations. Judgment in teaching has come in for some attention in the past. Mere facts have become suspect by those who work closely with their development and accumulation. Hearing the facts, knowing the facts, and understanding the facts are all important to teachers. Using the facts in an acceptable way, teaching pupils to develop warranted beliefs, application of concepts in a timely manner, and in general pushing beyond the rudiments of learning are within the realm of moving from an average teacher to the heights of powerful teaching.

Whether a teacher obtains more formal college education which carries credit and leads to degrees is not as important in the enhancement of his power to teach as that he changes or improves his "stock in trade" which becomes available with which to help his students in the future. Taking a course for no credit, or auditing a course, or reading a book or taking a trip, or going to church, or going to a psychiatrist or a medical doctor, or getting married, or buying his own home might work to the advantage of his future students. Just reading the newspapers and periodicals regularly and intelligently would probably contribute to a teacher's potential for helping his pupils. Strictly speaking, whatever helps the teacher to develop his values, adjust himself both emotionally and socially, develop and maintain his physical and mental health, acquire new interests, understand his pupils and all young people better, acquire new insights into the learning process, gain experience in trouble-shooting youth and children's problems, become able to use new methods of teaching intelligently, and grow in the knowledge of his major discipline — all of these, and more, will enhance a teacher's power to forever influence his pupils.

ENHANCING TEACHING POWER THROUGH PSYCHOLOGICAL OWNERSHIP

Just as in other enterprises, the owner is assumed to take more pride in and exert more efforts than an employee to increase the enterprise's effectiveness and profits so, too, in teaching this principle applies. If the schools belong to the people, as the legend has it, then it would appear that worry over effectiveness and merit would attach itself to the "owners." If the public through the unique arrangement of electing its own representatives (members of boards of education) and turning the education of children over to them, divests itself of the responsibility for teaching effectiveness, then the boards must find someone to delegate this responsibility to in order that it may be effectively discharged. Here the chief school administrator comes in. As the executive secretary to the board, the superintendent finds himself the key person through delegation of authority and responsibility to exercise the leadership in teaching effectiveness. And, of course, there are several ways in which this has been traditionally carried out. First in the selection of teachers, the superintendent tries to choose those who have teaching potential for greatness and to avoid those who would not be effective under the local situation. Then, later on in the assignment to duty, delegation of additional responsibilities, and supervision of teaching performance, numerous doors to helping the teacher live up to his highest potential are opened. But one thing is missing. If the teacher, who admittedly has the potential, does not settle down into an attitude of "This is my school" but hangs onto the "they" concept, all the time considering the position as just another way of making a living, then the chance for enhancement of teaching power is severely limited. Actually the "our school" attitude is superior to the "my school" as the teamwork concept is implied. Then the team can be effective with credit to the entire team rather than to any one in particular. Each in his own way, and with particular contributions, can make effective education available to the pupils. And by working together, sharing ideas, and putting the welfare of the pupils as the supreme rule of the school, the highest possible effectiveness will be achieved which will reflect on each and every member of the faculty. It is here that the "faculty family" concept is developed with each having specific responsibilities which add up to a whole which, from the student's point of view, is entirely sufficient to take care of his learning needs in a highly effective manner.

The psychological ownership of a school situation which is admittedly actually owned by the public, staffed by agents of society, and enjoyed by the sons and daughters of all the people, is an experience in intellectual idealism which pays rich dividends to all concerned. It is one of the surest ways to develop teaching power on the part of a young, inexperienced teacher who has determined that he will develop his potential with all possible speed. It is an attitude of promise, it inevitably leads to an arrangement approaching the perfection described as "If other things were equal, I would..." because the holder of the psychological ownership theory works like a Trojan to make his dream come true. The concept puts the foundation under the dreams of the teacher who proceeds to build the superstructure and become a great influence in the lives of his students.

ENHANCING TEACHING POWER THROUGH PLACEMENT

The concept of placement relates to where the teacher takes a position. Just as in any other situations in life, there may be built-in conditions in a given position which would work for the success or the failure of a given teacher. The wise teacher knows his own defects and limitations, and so if it is at all possible, carefully rejects those situations where the spotlight of attention would focus on his weaknesses. Then, too, there are the facts of professional life connected with the administration, supervision and human relations of a given position. In determining where a person can do his best work much study should be given to the various factors which might contribute to or detract from the chances and opportunities to be effective and to become increasingly so. In the history of American education, much of the placement has been of economic or geographical determination, or by accident of openings at the moment. This, without regard to where a person could turn in the best possible performance and grow in teaching power while on the job. Dead-end positions have been taken by many who lived to regret the moves.

Alert, forward looking placement directors are increasingly trying to match the applicant to the position where the performance will be effective from the beginning and where the other personnel, the community, and all other factors will permit the teacher to become increasingly effective with prompt recognition and reward as expectations. Placement officials have become increasingly aware that promising young teachers need to be reminded to move to other positions where opportunities for improvement are available to them in order to avoid getting into the rut of anonymity and relative ineffectiveness for a person of high caliber and potential teaching power.

ENHANCING TEACHING POWER THROUGH ASSIGNMENT

Once a position has been taken, the exact assignment to duty is of extreme importance if the teacher is to demonstrate how much teaching merit he has. To load promising classroom teachers down with myriad routine assignments without room for growth or opportunity to prove merit is to misassign a teacher. Many examples of misassignment could be given. Bad assignments which prevent a teacher from demonstrating just how good he could be in the instructional area are also to be avoided. Thousands of otherwise wonderful teachers have been shunted off into the morass of unchallenging assignments to serve out their days and thus rob their pupils of the best that they could do.

Assignments in recent years have tended to be in terms of responsibilities, rather than in strict terms of classes to be taught, committee assignments, and other routine chores. Teachers who wish to exhibit their qualitative approach to teaching are usually given not only permission to do so, but wide latitude within specific responsibilities to prove themselves. As proof of results come in, administration officials are prone to provide more and more leeway for effective teachers to carry out their teaching responsibilities in the most effective way the teacher can discover. This has brought about such innovations as team teaching, and numerous experimental procedures on various levels, not the least effective of which has been the case study and incident process techniques.

Before an assignment can be made on the basis of individual competence, the assignor should have some information and evidence. The question of who is best where and why has largely been left to chance or the subjective judgment of the administration.

ENHANCING TEACHING POWER THROUGH ADMINISTRATION

The greatest responsibility of administrators is to help a teacher improve his teaching. Whereas, at one time the administrator was a teacher and officially described as the headmaster or head teacher, now, typically, superintendents do not teach and more and more principals do not teach very much if at all. Their existence is completely justified if they, through their efforts, make possible better teaching on the part of the classroom teachers. Actually, shielding teachers from many routine tasks and interferences is a wonderful contribution to teaching efficiency. There are more direct and effective ways of assisting teachers, however.

Selection of well-qualified teachers and recommending their employment to the Board of Education, assignment to duty so that the teacher can do his best work, counseling with the teacher from time to time on problems involving administration of the school, carrying the burden of correspondence, reporting, and public relations in the formal sense, all indicate possibilities of the school administration to assist the classroom teacher improve the quality of his teaching. Understanding and encouragement of teachers in their dealing with the real problems of instruction is within the province of the principal and superintendent in most systems.

The faculty as a whole is as weak as its poorest instructor. Power in teaching from the over-all faculty point of view would seem to be responsive to the will of the chief administrator and the teacher-employing authorities. If they are interested in quality or excellence in education, they will replace weak links in the chain with strong and potentially strong ones. A teacher once was asked how the superintendent and board could improve instruction in his courses. His answer was direct and to the point: "Get a better teacher!" Another way would be to help teachers do their very best.

ENHANCING TEACHING POWER THROUGH LEAVES OF ABSENCE

It has long been taken for granted that a teacher who takes a leave of absence, whether sabbatical or regular, should come back to his teaching job with renewed energy and greater determination to do a better job than ever he possessed before. Students have a right to expect more powerful and valuable teaching from the teacher back from a leave. Even if the teacher traveled around the world, never earning a single hour of credit in his discipline, the expectation is high that he will be a better teacher. By this, we imply that he will be more able to assist pupils with their needs and problems than ever he was before.

The basic theory behind granting leaves of absence would seem to imply acquisition of renewed strength, new ideas for use with pupils, new perspectives, and above all else, growth in over-all teaching power. This narrow concept causes some boards and governing bodies to reject applications for sabbatical leaves when it is clear from the application itself that such a result would not be forthcoming. Ordinary leaves, at the expense of the teacher, would not as a rule be prescribed by governing boards but at least, the period of time granted should not see a reduction of teaching power potential on the part of the teacher. Reasons of health or family emergencies cause some teachers to apply for leave for repairing deficiencies or making arrangements which will leave the teacher relatively free to pursue his teaching with full force which would not be the case had the leave not been granted.

Regardless of the type of leave, pupils have a right to expect better teaching when the teacher returns from a leave.

PRE-SERVICE PREPARATION

Without a good background of pre-service preparation, no teacher is likely to be as powerful as he might otherwise be. The best preparation is none too good for a person who aspires to become an outstanding teacher. Just as in everything else, life has its price for what it gives us. The price of a strong preparation to teach is years of hard work and developmental activities leading to readiness to commence. There are never any finished products either at the end of college or at the end of a career in teaching.

Thinkers in the field of teacher education see the need for a broad background of liberal arts, or as it is more generally referred to, of general education. How this acts as a foundation to a teacher is explained as education in scope with the special preparation in what and how to teach as the education in depth. But since a teacher is an actor with many roles to play, any and all of his pre-service preparation will find usefulness in one or more of his roles beyond teaching. These roles cover his citizenship on the local, state, national and international levels; his relationships with his church, his family, his friends, his clubs, and his professional organizations; and not the least by any means is the area of human relations with his pupils, fellow teachers, administrators, parents, taxpayers, government officials, and critics of education.

The task of the pre-service preparers is so gigantic that they are demanding and getting in some places an extra year or two for the purpose of developing the best potential in candidates for the teaching profession. This at least gives promising candidates for teaching every opportunity to prepare themselves for a life of service wherein they can demonstrate ableness and promise right from the beginning of their careers. The combination of a great classroom teacher and a competent research scholar in a candidate for a teaching position would ordinarily insure teaching power. But the opposite would also work very well, that is, a great scholar and a competent teacher would also very likely influence students throughout their lives. Either combination would appear to be promising so far as students are concerned.

METHODS OF TEACHING

The archer of old who had but one arrow in his quiver was likely to be in for trouble unless he was a marksman par excellence and the right breaks came his way. So teachers with but one teaching technique are severely limited in their operations. Today with teaching every bit as complex as the practice of medicine in all of its phases, the diagnoses, therapy, and follow-up procedures, we need as many techniques, procedures, tactics, and plans for action as we can find. Depending on the sources of information, one can find thirty to forty recognized patterns of teaching described and recommended. The powerful teacher knows about many and is careful to use a variety of approaches so as to capture the imagination and enlist the support of each of his pupils and he is careful not to neglect the real needs of given individuals who might profit from one method and not another which was being used by his classmates.

Methods contribute proximately to the artistry and power of a teacher and make palatable the heavy doses of hard work entailed in the learning process. Every teacher knows that there is no royal road to learning and furthermore that there might be many trails and passages to goals where no one wide kingsway sweeps away to its destination. For one, a direct route may be indicated while for others more devious ways must be planned in the light of their apperceptive mass of background experiences and the fact that they do not see the goal nor perceive the direction in which they are traveling. So a teacher must of necessity know of all the possible roads leading to the selected destination, mark out the journey, and counsel with each learner on what would seem for him to be the best in point of economy of time and permanence of learning for a lifetime of use.

As a practical approach to enhancing teaching power, a teacher would be well advised to develop his own teaching personality in terms of manner, style, and approach. Within administrative flexibility and academic freedom, most teachers have the widest possible latitude for normal evolution and professional growth into competent teachers who can and who will powerfully influence their pupils. Just as an idea may become so powerful in the life of a person that it kills or replaces its rivals and literally dominates behavior, so a powerful teacher can change young human lives in radically wonderful ways. Teachers who assume positions of such great influence in the lives of their students would not understand subject matter to be sanctified but to be used as a means to an end. Nor would they hold that there is one "best" method. Extremely valuable insights and concepts are gained through demonstrations, experiments, research and the re-checking of experiences of other teachers in realistic situations.

This generation's teachers who wield considerable power over their former pupils have achieved excellence largely on or through their own efforts and not as a result of close supervision of other teachers. Self exploitation of his own mistakes and successes provides a threat-free possibility for a teacher. Avoidance of stifling a teacher's creative attempts to enhance his teaching power is a "must" for administrators. Such explorations, innovations, experimental rallies, demonstrations of individuality and fresh approaches to problem situations all point to development of power potential. The same challenging freedom exercised by the teacher is likely to capture the imagination and inspire the student to look toward taking up the challenge of self-directive responsibility and all the stimulation and other rewards this entails.

Perhaps the greatest single cause of powerless teaching and learning is best described as aimless teaching and learning. Going through the motions of teaching-learning, filling up the teaching-learning space, spending the time in "talking and listening" are not the qualifications for powerful teaching and learning. It may be that the teacher who teaches the best, teaches the least so that his students can be aroused to self-activity because of genuine learning motivation based on honest mental, cultural, economic, and inspirational values truly and presently apparent.

One of the finest statements on improvement of teaching is to be found in Mayer's writings. He writes:

> Teaching involves self-examination. Without it, we repeat the same course year after year and our lectures and discussions become mechanical exercises. Without it, we never develop genuine depth and we become intellectual Pharisees. Without it, we mistake academic appearance for inward learning. We should ask such questions as:
>
> Am I reaching the student?
>
> Am I conveying the main ideas of the subject which I am teaching?
>
> Am I developing lasting interests?
>
> Am I encouraging independent thinking?

Am I developing in my students an affirmative view of life?

Am I making them more restless and dissatisfied with mediocrity?

Am I imbuing them with a sense of intellectual adventure?[15]

The teacher who can answer these questions in the affirmative is or will become a powerful teacher.

The teacher who "teaches" or merely runs through subject-matter of a course but declines to personally apply or use what he is teaching, that is, he has no true commitment to action, does not intend to demonstrate personally what he is urging his pupils to learn, takes the "so what?" attitude, certainly reveals a professional sickness and needs help. If he is to remain in teaching, therapy is indicated so that he may engage in constant self-examination and acquisition of new knowledge along with its application. Such a person should move from new knowledge to behavioral changes which heighten activities for improvements in teaching.

Similarly, the student who "learns" or merely becomes familiar with materials of a course but declines to apply or use what he has learned, that is, he has absolutely no commitment to action by reason of enrolling in the course, does not intend to use what he learns, takes the "so what?" attitude, demonstrates beyond doubt an academic sickness and needs help immediately. Therapy is indicated if constant self-examination and acquisition of new knowledge do not lead to changes and heightened activity for improved behavior on the part of the student.

While the growth of knowledge in former times was slow and slight, it has now become rapid and great. Such a development confronts both teachers who wish to become increasingly effective and students who really want to learn all they can in the shortest possible time. Such considerations have a bearing on teaching power and style as well as learning techniques and motivation.

Commenting on the attempts to keep up and teach in the latest approved fashion, President Eliot is quoted as saying:

The rapidity with which methods of instruction and fields of instruction change from generation to generation, and even from decade to decade, is one of the most astonishing facts in the history of education. Thus there is not a single subject within the whole range of instruction at Harvard University, from the beginning of the undergraduate course to the end of the graduate courses, which is now taught in the same way in which it was taught forty years ago, or which offers the same field of instruction which was offered to the students of the last generation. All the methods and apparatus of teaching, and the spirit or temper of teacher and taught alike, have changed. Some of these profound changes begin in the faculties; but others begin outside the university in the working world, and must be discerned, appreciated, and adapted by the faculties; some are university inventions; but many are the consequences of social, industrial and political changes in the outside world. Every faculty, therefore, has to keep up with the rapid march of educational events, and for this purpose it must have frequent stated meetings, and patient discussions of new proposals.[16]

The real purpose of a school is to "catalyze genuine self-education" as Paul Douglass puts it.[17] Cantor alleges that "all genuine learning in the final analysis is self-education."[18] Despite what many teachers and students appear to believe about the lecture, it is not given for the purpose of informing them but "rather to compel them to inquire and discover for themselves."[19]

TEACHER'S HEALTH

Any observer in the field of education can relate how a once powerful teacher deteriorated under the heavy hand of disease or process of aging conditions. Any of the usual illnesses impair a teacher's power to teach on a temporary basis and it should be known to all concerned that it is not fair to anyone involved in the enterprise to permit a teacher who is not able to bear the great responsibilities of teaching to carry on as if he were fully able. To do so is no kindness to anyone — especially the teacher and the pupils.

PERSONAL EXAMPLE AND QUALITIES

The personal qualities of a teacher find expression in the type of example which he gives to his pupils. If these qualities are admired and enjoyed by pupils, then the teacher has a reasonably good chance to exercise much influence upon his pupils through model behavior. If on the other hand, his example is abhorred, this will mitigate against whatever else he strives to teach so that his teaching power quotient will be quite low.

In a stirring passage on the responsibilities and obligations of a teacher who would exert a powerful influence, the Educational Policies Commission claims that:

> The first responsibility of the teacher is to maintain a steadfast and informed loyalty to the values and processes of democracy, to the several articles of the democratic faith, to the interests of children and the cause of human freedom. He should see clearly that education is more than subject matter, that education is fundamentally an adventure in human relationships. He should see too the far-reaching social, political and moral implications and consequences of all that he undertakes. In the work of the school and in the life of the community he should exemplify the spirit of democracy. He should struggle without ceasing to apply the articles of this great faith to both education and society. He should be among the first to sense violations of the principles of democracy, to apply these principles to neglected fields, to keep alight the lamps of reason, to champion the interests of the underprivileged and the downtrodden, to combat the forces of totalitarianism, whether of domestic or foreign origin — to make democracy work. In a word, he should take democracy seriously and strive to make it prevail in the world, giving himself fully to its service and enlisting at every opportunity the energies and enthusiasms of his pupils. An example of democracy in his own life, he would exert upon the young a powerful and lasting influence for human freedom.[20]

It takes a certain personality to be able to work effectively with children, youth and young adults. The qualities of living they admire, the personal example they would like, and the activities of the teacher might not be in fullest agreement with the wishes of the pupils' parents. As an intermediary between the generations, between the past and the future, between the institution and the chosen discipline, between the heritage of the present and the hopes of the future in addition to the common agent of the current clientele and of society at large, the teacher is in a thoroughly untenable position for personal maximum enjoyment without hindrance of his own private life. It is really no different from life in a goldfish bowl, or performing services which surely cannot ever be pleasing to all concerned, that is the paymasters, the recipients, the regulators, and the laborers themselves. Sensible as teachers are, they do have minds and lives of their own and are entitled to some protection from over-exposure in their own private lives and exhibition of personal qualities.

The examples and qualities of teacher performances are directly related to teaching power. Either they enhance or they detract from what it otherwise would be.

SUPERVISION OF INSTRUCTION

There are many authorities in the field of supervision of instruction. These people have effectively demonstrated that "A man's purpose is the soul of his writing." The unique value of a supervisor of instruction within a school is that with his help, the teachers can do a better job of teaching than would otherwise be possible. Just as Briggs believed that teachers should help pupils to do better the desirable things that they would ordinarily do, and help them raise their sights in addition, so the supervisor of instruction offers this valuable service to teachers and along the same lines. What the teacher is to the pupil, so the supervisor could be to the teacher — a friendly helper in the important work at hand. If two heads are better than one in achieving a common purpose, then a supervisor is adding to a teacher's power to achieve by becoming his counselor, his assistant, his co-worker and his friend.

A supervisor who takes his job seriously will oftentime find that the teachers who aspire to becoming powerful teachers will welcome their help while others who have no such aspiration will reject supervision right from the beginning. In one sense, the presence of a supervisor is some test of the future outlook and current ambitions of teachers in the way classroom teachers view the service which is there to help them become increasingly more powerful.

We see the supervisory activity but not much improvement of teaching. Neither, as in evolution, where the process goes on incessantly, is there much proof that the effectiveness of teachers is either higher or lower by reason of the type of supervision provided for classroom teachers. Here and there, we recognize a great teacher but in no case can the greatness be traced to the work of a supervisor. If supervision is not the answer, what then is the key to greatness in the classroom?

TEACHING POWER AND CREATIVITY

In all of our thinking about teaching power, we must not forget that our chief concern is with the ultimate outcome of teaching, that is the use made of the products of learning. If a teacher and pupils, working together, can develop new knowledge, skills, understandings, attitudes, and appreciations, then the human creative spirit has achieved at least the first step in the direction of teaching power.

Students who have not yet developed a sincere appreciation for their precious heritage as learners have certainly neglected their own education and apparently have been neglected by their parents and teachers. Similarly, those who did not prepare adequately for the responsibilities of adult life, or who do not live up to the level of their intellectual endowment, have neglected important areas of life and been neglected by those who should have helped in these matters. Why was more adequate instruction not supplied while yet there was time? And while questions are being asked, why is much of the traditional school program far removed from the real concerns of enrollees? Why, indeed, are both teachers and pupils so terribly complacent about education if not genuinely not interested in it other than as a present burden? And, why, oh why, are honest interpretative results of school achievements not brought to the attention of both pupils and their parents in a forceful fashion to jar them out of their lethargy? To conceive of the curriculum as something the school offers is not an adequate concept. It is more. It more properly can concern itself descriptively with what the learners do in the way of their values, their needs, their genuine experiences, things which are truly meaningful now and will forever integrate themselves into their very being. Going to school to influential teachers is another way of saying that a learner is broadening and enhancing his experiences, and learning how to grow continuously in the power to live a rich and full life in a kindly, sympathetic environment which he is helping to create and shape. Furthermore, a teacher who has the autonomy to develop real teaching power, can help his students improve the quality of their meanings, values, sentiments, and whatever else goes into their own self-development. He can help them to avoid their own shortcomings and weaknesses and improve the quality of their thinking, their own self-image, their career plans and probably, as important as any of these, he can maximize the probability of their dreams coming to realization.

Is there a connection between teaching power and creativity in students? The effective teacher becomes the co-creator of the quality of creativeness in his students. But to do this the teacher must be truly creative, that is, he must be the block from which the chips fall.

Powerful teaching takes into consideration that the highest act of creativity is self-fulfillment. Both teaching and learning have important parts in this process. For teaching is a direct avenue to self-fulfillment for the teacher who seeks to make the arrangements so that his students may come into their own self-fulfillment. No greater joy is ever forthcoming to a teacher than to see the creative process take hold of a student to the point of possessing him and moving him on toward his own self-fulfillment. No teacher sacrifice is too great for this return which dwarfs such considerations as salary, prestige, and others of lesser importance.

Teaching power is another way of indicating instructional effectiveness. In one way or another, each person is a teacher, and as such has a teaching power quotient. No one has ever come up with an acceptable or even accurate measuring instrument for this important ability. Perhaps they never will. To increase in one's power to teach is indeed a great accomplishment. Human progress and the welfare of mankind hinge on the degree to which the race learns lessons from its accumulated knowledge and applies these learnings.

Teaching power or effectiveness in one sense reflects both previous and future performance, the measure of which is hard to take because of the time interval complication. Evaluation awaits the day, when figuratively speaking, the seed (teaching) shall have germinated, grow and develop, flower, and bear its own fruit (action) in the life of the learner. As St. Paul of the Bible has said, "hope by its very nature, implies a period of waiting." The relationship of teacher power to style is assumed to be intriguingly close. Alter the style, and the teaching power is likely to be substantially influenced.

From the standpoint of non-personal qualities, good teachers can be more powerful teachers when they have plenty of materials with which to work, and are blessed with students who really want to learn. In an analysis of good teaching, Alexander and Halverson have identified ten significant characteristics which might well serve as guidelines for teachers seeking to multiply their teaching power. They are:

1. The maintenance of an atmosphere, social and physical, in the classroom which stimulates and encourages problem-solving activity.
2. The functioning of the teacher as a guide and helper rather than as a taskmaster and dictator.
3. The encouragement of friendly and efficient sharing and cooperation in all phases of classroom activity.
4. The use, so far as feasible, of pupils' own motives as guides in the selection of learning goals and experiences.
5. Careful understanding of and attention to the needs of individual learners.
6. Patterns of group organization which utilize fully group influences on learning.
7. The use of evaluative processes and devices to help learners make optimum progress.

8. Emphasis on and respect for accomplishment in the acquisition of understandings and skills needed by learners in solving problems attacked in learning situations.
9. Adequate and definite plans and resources for instruction which insure desirable learning experiences and permit flexibility in the classroom development of plans.
10. Use of an experimental approach that continually seeks better procedures and also evidence regarding the effectiveness of procedures tried.[21]

Ayer, in discussing supervision of instruction, makes some incisive comments about good teaching.

> Learning at its best is the process of discovery by oneself. Teaching at its best is the stimulation and direction of learning. Both learning and teaching are exacting and satisfying.
>
> The good teacher is a partner of and a companion to the learner. The artist teacher may be described as a personnel adviser in the realm of human behavior, reflecting the spirit of faithful accuracy characteristic of the scholar combined with the pulsating sympathy of the good parent.
>
> Effective learning and teaching demand mutual understanding between learner and teacher. The inspirational teacher is characterized by patience, explanation, wonderment, and challenging inquiry. But inspirational teaching requires deep and wide scholarship of subject matter diversified skills in presentation.[22]

And Wiles, also in the field of supervision says that:

> Creative teaching involves being dissatisfied with the results obtained with present procedures, feeling that perfection is something never quite attained but constantly sought, having new ideas, being willing to try the new ideas and to evaluate the results produced. Creativeness is really a constant state of experimentation.[23]

Chapter 5

Configurations of Teaching Power

The dimensions of the quality of a teacher's control over others are not easy to describe. The outlines, fashions, shapes and degrees of power are, nevertheless, present in the usual teacher-pupil relationships. In given situations, perhaps the only accurate assessment of the influence exerted would come through a specific case study designed to study the contours, evaluate the quality, and report on the effects.

In this connection, it is worth noting that while the indispensable key to teaching power lies with the teacher, important clues to both teaching and learning effectiveness lie with pupils. For though as we shall shortly look at teaching power indicators in the make-up of teachers, we should never overlook the important factors of student politics, religion, accumulated experiences, capacity to learn, sophistication, socio-economic status and outlook, — all of which tend to predispose a student to receive teacher influence with various degrees of effect, immediacy, intermediacy, and ultimacy.

The community of scholars consists of both scholar-teachers as well as scholar-pupils. One aspect of a school's teaching power certainly lies in the power to attract to itself the certain type of student which is maximally susceptible to the unique thrust of the particular community of scholars — both faculty and students alike. It is appropriate for young learners with specific interests and needs to seek admission to schools which specialize in the main areas of their concern. If this is a key to teaching power, it is certainly understandable and commendable for both the institution, with its faculty on the one hand, and the pupil population on the other. Such selection does not insure or guarantee teaching power, but it sets the scene for maximum and mutual influence to be exerted within the community. In interpreting such situations, one would be compelled to conclude that neither the school's faculty nor the students could claim greatness without the other. This, then is one facet of teaching power — and perhaps the *main* one. Stated briefly, it would be:

The basis of teaching power whether in an institution as a whole, a department or division, or on the part of a teaching team or single individual, is to be discovered in the relationship which develops and exists between the teacher and the taught. As a developmental construct, the relationship mentioned is a tool of thought which can be deliberately used in gaining both orientation in teaching power and truly configurational method of functioning as a teacher. The outline of power can be traced from the relationship as it develops.

From the standpoint of success, posture or "stance" is not the most important factor in obtaining an education. It has been said that going to school is easy but getting an education is hard. Just being in school is but the initial formal step which might be described as the posture of education but there is more to it than just being present where teaching and learning are going on. It takes active participation and dogged determination to "try, try again" until mastery comes for the elementary and advanced concepts needed by the individual for his own future welfare and success. Inimical to true scholarly progress are such things as procrastination, poor budgeting of time and resources, neglect of health, faulty methodology, inability to use the library effectively, and failure to exploit opportunities for wide interpersonal relationship possibilities. The old bromide of "It's not what you know but whom you know" is not entirely accurate yet it points up the folly of not cultivating friendships while opportunities to do so are present.

POSTURES OF POWER OF TEACHERS

In the centuries that man has traveled, the mores of social organization and control have grown into the consciousness of even the very young. In connection with the physical postures of teachers and their pupils, a casual observer would note the great freedom enjoyed by the teacher while the pupils had only as much freedom of movement as it pleased the teacher to grant to them. Then, the observer would normally see that the teacher characteristically stood much of the time while the pupils sat hour after hour. In the early years, pupils were commanded to lie down for short periods of time but the teacher did not also lie down with them. On short trips, the teacher might either lead the procession to show the way or bring up the rear of the column to keep a protective eye on the situation.

Rank and power are intimately associated with the postures of social behavior. The teacher who permits or commands his pupils to group themselves in alphabetical order while seated, or sit where they choose, or form a semi-circle facing the teacher, or completely encircle the teacher is telling much about himself and his understanding of the role of the teacher. For who can contradict the assumption that the teacher who stands always before the class whose members are always seated, has a different understanding of the significance of power posture than the teacher who characteristically drifts to the back of the room, or the one who patrols the aisles, or seats himself among the pupils leaving the front of the room without a central authority figure? Can we not deduce the amount of authority the teacher desires for himself from a study of his physical posture and movements within the classroom situation?

Occasionally, one sees a teacher who sits on a raised platform or one who has had a special speaker's stand constructed for his use. In some older classrooms the teacher's chair was so built with high back, arms, and other feature as to approach the throne of a king. This coupled with an elevated deck clearly exposes the authority role of the teacher who from his position and stance views his subjects from his kingly demesne. One needs also to remember that the day of pupils all standing when a teacher enters the room is not in the distant past. What a revelation this action is! To greet the teacher with one voice as he arrives is also enlightening. To await the seating of the teacher before any of the pupils may be re-seated is significant. One could go on and on in this enumeration of the configurations of teaching power. It might be noted that evidences of such practices are not confined to any one level but find outlets in various places, all levels, and are even cherished and taught in the name of courtesy and good manners in some schools.

One occasionally sees relics of the days gone by when the silent configurations of power evidenced themselves in postures of humans in their church activities, military customs, governmental functions, and family traditions. The kneeling, standing, sitting, use of elevated floors, and personal prostrations all tell the story of power status and its use in dealing with other human beings. "We know what it means," says Canetti, "when one man sits raised up while everyone round him stand; when one man stands and everyone else sits; when everyone in a room gets up as someone comes in; when one man falls on his knees before another; when a new arrival is not asked to sit down."[1]

RIGHTS AND POWERS

No clear cut line of demarcation has ever apparently been made between a teacher's power and a teacher's rights. None of the powers enumerated above are thought to be rights in the true sense of the word. Even the so-called "right to punish" a pupil is not really a right even though it may be within the power of the teacher. The making of assignments would not constitute a "right" in the true sense, either.

What are the rights of the teacher? Chief among them is the right to freedom of action so that the best possible results may be obtained. This is sometimes referred to as academic freedom or freedom to teach. Other rights might be to select appropriate methods for use in the instructional process, to develop a style of teaching which is peculiarly fitting, to the freedoms guaranteed to all Americans, to participate actively in professional organizations, to have access to the services of the school available to other teachers, and a right to a living and a saving income for professional services rendered. All of these impinge upon the powers of the teacher to influence the lives of pupils. As such, these rights would appear to be the foundation upon which the potential powers of a teacher are based. Without exercise of the rights, no effective use of teaching power would seem possible.

DUTIES AND POWERS

Just as in the case of the rights and powers, so a teacher has, by virtue of the position he has assumed in society and further by reason of his contractual status, certain specific duties and responsibilities devolving upon him. It might be easy to confuse his powers with his duties but, here again, there is a distinction to be made between them. It is the duty of the teacher to prepare himself for a life of service to his community and his prospective pupils, to specifically prepare himself for instructional functions, to become the leader in the learning situation, to keep the records and tell the truth about the progress made in learning for his students. It is his duty to plan for all of the contingencies of the instructional situation and to cooperate with other teachers and with administrators in the over-all planning of the school enterprise. On a lower level, it is the duty of the teacher to arrive promptly at school, sign in if this is the practice, take the roll, grade papers if necessary, and counsel with students who desire personal advice relating to their school work. It is the duty of a teacher to communicate promptly with his superiors in matters of interest to them. There is no escape from the duties involved in teaching while in the exercise of powers there are options and alternatives almost completely within the province of the teacher. In the matter of duties, external influences acting as force dictate the conditions of teacher behavior and set up standards for evaluation. Not so in the exercise of powers where the action of the teacher could only be collated with that of reasonably prudent teachers who found themselves in similar circumstances and then a wide latitude of outcomes would be tolerated and looked upon as perfectly acceptable under the circumstances.

DEGREES OF UTILIZATION OF POWERS AND TEACHING POWER

Beyond carrying out to the extent personally desired in the areas of his rights and to the extent his superiors desired in the area of his duties, a teacher is called upon to exercise his powers in the direction and control of the teaching-learning process at every possible point. Hardly a class period arrives without some evidence of the exercise of such powers on the part of the teacher, or evidence of the effects of such usage in the lives of his pupils. Most teachers and pupils could, on reflection, recall the situations when a teacher had elected to use his powers in a particular way. In some cases, the entire group of learners was the recipient, while in others, individuals were singled out to be the recipients.

It has been observed to be true that some teachers rarely if ever use their powers in certain areas and make no attempt to apply uniformly whatever powers they possess. In other words, some teachers specialize in the display of one power, neglecting what other powers they might have, while their fellow teachers would emphasize other powers. This throws a peculiar burden on students who must somehow get to know the situation before entering classes or else suffer for a time at least the peculiar bias of the teacher in the exercise of teaching power. Since pupils do have a half dozen or so teachers at the elementary level, and probably twice that number at the secondary level with twenty-five or more at the higher level, this matter of understanding the proneness to power tactics of given teachers becomes a real problem in the selection of courses and the planning of programs. Counselors and advisors are fully aware of this situation and do what they can to inform and alleviate the situation in advance.

FORMS OF TEACHING POWER

The forms of teaching power as observed in American schools in the latter half of the Twentieth century might be described as relating to rewards, punishments, prescriptions, identifications, and acceptances. In addition to these powers, all teachers have certain rights and duties which form the foundation for the exercise of their powers which find expression in direct influences leading to changes in the lives of their pupils. In the following treatment of these powers, their setting and structure will be described along with examples and forms, present and future values, costs to students, by-products of application, and evaluation of their relative effect on pupils.

POWER TO REWARD

Teaching power is one form of social power. Its magnitude has never been measured with accuracy but rather has been evaluated subjectively by those who perceive it in operation far beyond the momentary and fleeting changes which occur during the teaching process per se. Power because of its nature must necessarily be defined in terms of influence, and influence in terms of changes which occur in the lives of learners. Of course, as with many other human situations, it is well that we remember that multiple causation is not only possible but probable in explanation of long range changes in pupils.

Taken together, the forms of teacher power provides a configuration of the influences and changes initiated in the classroom but which through delayed action come to fulfillment later on in life. It is also obvious that a concomitant outcome of teaching power is the current teacher "force" which operates for the moment and is gone with the passing of the temporary roles of the teacher and pupils. When the external arrangement for school is dissolved, then the accompanying force evaporates. Of course, many with desire and delight wish to prolong such a relationship of force over the years and through sentimental memories enjoy it forever. But inevitably the force disappears and then comes the true test of teaching power — that influence that leads to actual changes even though the force be removed and forgotten.

When a student perceives that his teacher has the power to obtain a reward for him, he brings himself within the power of the teacher insofar as the teacher's influence and power to change behavior are concerned. When the teacher realizes that it is within his power to mediate rewards to his pupils, he is on his way to extending his power over his pupils. Mutual understanding of this possibility and acceptance of it as an instructional modus vivendi lead to the extension of teaching power not only in class situations and out of class situations here and now but to future changes in behavior as well.

Whether it is within the power of a teacher to offer rewards to pupils is somewhat within the province of his pupils to say.

It may be that nothing the teacher can offer will be acceptable and thus nothing that would qualify as a reward is available. On the other hand, it is conceivable that what pupils really want is not within the realm of the possible for a teacher to give. Aside from the selfish reasons which sometimes appear to supply the motive for either the giving or receiving of these rewards, the purposes and expectations of others than the teacher's own pupils enter into the situation. We refer here to parents, friends of pupils, and other teachers who are interested in the welfare and progress of students and who seek to assist them.

The acceptance or rejection of proffered rewards is for all practical purposes a part of the results of the relationship which forms the basis for teaching power. Most rewards are received in name if not in spirit although the in-name-only type of acceptance usually never brings an example of teaching power.

For a teacher to dangle cheap, tawdry prizes before the eyes of pupils is but to tantalize them. Most will not be able to resist the prize but will be unable or unwilling to deliver on the implied promise of bringing themselves under the power of the giver and thereby making themselves change under his influence. It may be a question of loving the gift but not the giver or a careful separation of the gift from the purpose for which it was given.

Rewards to pupils from teachers which have the effect of bringing pupils under the influence of a teacher on both the short and long term dimensions, range all the way from fleeting smiles to tangible awards in recognition of past performances or future promise. Among the in-betweens might fall the following: high grades, cooperation, compliments, selection for attention, recommendation for honors, expression of confidence in, indication of personal preferment, favorable attitude toward, partiality in personal dealings, and other evidences of special helpfulness. In none of the above situations is there an implication that there is anything amiss. No immorality, no question of ethics, no law breaking, no unfair practices are involved. As examples of teacher behavior, these rewards tend to bring the student under the power of teachers so that whatever the teacher wants the pupil to do, or be, or see, or not to do any of these things, then the pupil is, more than likely, eager and willing to conform without a second thought. The pupil is brought into an arrangement where he is indebted to the teacher for past favors — even if the belief is held that each and every one of them were earned.

What is the value to a student or to a teacher of a student's ready conformity to the desires of the instructor? Will the compliance, hard work, synthetic motivation, and all the other adjectival shorings of this influence of the teacher leave a permanent mark upon the pupil? Will it be an affirmative or positive vestige or will it be harmful? One rather obvious answer to such a question is that it all depends upon the kind of teacher and his rewards and the impact they have upon the personality of the pupil. It could work for a hypocritical interlude or for a genuine approach of stimulating excellence in learning. Sooner or later the pupil will have to understand that sincerity and practicality require rewards to relate themselves to pupil performance in the same way that artificial incentives lead on into reality when the medium can be removed without loss but rather with profit. Rewards should never be conceived of in the spirit of bribes or demanded as blackmail or for that matter continued with rank regularity until they became routine and lose their chief significance — extra returns for extra effort.

The cost to a pupil of receiving a reward from a teacher is not directly calculable but we can surmise that it is received with commensurate reduction of independence in future action. For when a reward is accepted, the influence of a teacher is thereby extended and the pupil either has changd already, is in process of doing so, or will in the future in direct relationship to the reward itself. It should be remembered that there is nothing immoral or unethical about influencing other people by mediating rewards for them. The teacher becomes the agent of society, the media through which the reward is obtained, not the prime giver. Clothed with authority to award such benefits as he sees fit in a circumspect manner, the teacher may be niggardly in this power or lavish in distribution of such favors. In any case, the recipient either has paid the price or will in the future. The matter is clear on this point. The teacher may not win any permanent friends by resorting to making such moves, but he will influence both friends and foes alike with a system of rewards. Not only are the pupils themselves changed but members of their family are substantially influenced by such rewards. It is interesting to note that from the standpoint of the teacher, disclaimer is usually made of any meritorious self-conduct. The matter is usually settled with "You deserved it or you wouldn't have gotten it." Pure unmerited favor and grace for a pupil singled out of a class would fall into the negative situation described below under the teacher's power to punish or coerce, in this case, all but the recipient of the unearned favor, who might be regarded as having equal right to the reward as the recipient.

The by-products of receiving a reward from a teacher ordinarily brings instant attraction from other pupils not so fortunate as the recipient of the grant. Whether there be jealousy or sincere mutual rejoicing is determined by other features of the class relationship and personality considerations. At any rate, such a reward is sure to focus attention on the recipient and especially so also on the teacher himself. Perhaps it gives new hope to non-recipients who may aspire for such rewards in the future. One thing it most certainly brings not only to the ones receiving the reward but to others equally and that is conformity to the wishes of the teacher. Such conformity could be somewhat insincere at times but nevertheless it is conformity for whatever reason. Time serving conformity will in the long run substantially influence the behavior of pupils through the development of thought patterns, deferment of courageous new actions, strengthening of habitual reactions, and the intellectual pattern of following rather than striking out in independence. Rewards substantially reduce dangers of rebellion in teacher-pupil relationships. And if there be enough to pass around to most if not all pupils in the group, and the award intervals are not too great, the natural tendency is to work for the rewards and wait in patience for the next interesting development. Teachers who use rewards for disciplinary control purposes sometimes make difficult the way of the teacher who does not also follow this procedure. If students develop the habit of expecting rewards and they are not forthcoming, then it can be realized that disappointment brings negative feelings which might again be classified as punishment rather than lack of rewards.

The power to reward originates not in the school but rather is brought to the school from home, from church, and from society in general. While it is believed to be salutary and good in general, it needs to be studied and administered in a judicious manner if it is to remain meaningful in most school situations. Otherwise, the unrealistic situation will arise where great expectations on the part of students can never be satisfied.

There can be no doubt but that suitable rewards tend to strengthen the bonds of friendship and to extend the power of a teacher to influence and change his pupils over relative long periods of time. But these rewards should be appropriate for the pupils in points of maturity and carefully calculated to provide natural motivating power to further education in an increasingly independent manner. After all, the teacher cannot remain around always to offer the rewards and neither can the pupils remain as immature learners whose outlook on life can be altered by such awards from time to time.

POWER TO PUNISH

Teaching power may be generated by the pupil's expectation that if he fails to conform to the teacher's influence attempt that he will be punished. In the true sense of the word, this is a self-induced coercion. Generated by fear that he will appear to reject the announced objectives of the teacher where he, the pupil, is concerned, the relationship has within it a negative quality which brings the learner under the control of the teacher who for all practical purposes may exert the maximum potential ability to influence the psychological behavior of his pupils without even wishing to play this role. Nevertheless, the pupil's opinions, attitudes, goals, needs, values and thoughts are colored with the comprehension of the power relationship which exists through no fault of either party to the arrangement. This range of power exists by virtue of society's sanctions, of the necessary and usual powers of direction belonging to the teaching profession, and with the concurrence of students who voluntarily welcome this means of learning. This is not to say that pupils who fall under the coercive power of a teacher do not reserve for themselves the necessary latitude of disagreement with what actually occurs. It is common knowledge that learners acquiesce in public but dissent in private on many developments in their school work. Likewise, their overt behavior does not always agree with the covert. As one student phrased it, we were as calm as icebergs outwardly in class but seething as volcanoes within over what happened. It might be observed here that teachers characteristically exercise great behavioral control over pupils but this is accompanied with only minor opinion control.

Whereas reward power if exercised judiciously leads to independence, the power to punish as it is usually applied to pupils normally leads to dependence. The fear that first brought pupils under the sway of a punishing teacher also acts as a great deterrent to independent endeavor. This is so because of the danger of displeasing the teacher still more than if nothing had been attempted. How often pupils prefer to wait upon the teacher to brief them in detail before starting learning tasks under fear of penalty if they move out on their own initiative. Coercive power oftentimes calls forth covert assistance from the colleagues of the punished in an attempt to divert the attention of the teacher and thus spare the pitied recipient of the teacher's wrath. It is not unusual for some sort of honor code to dictate to groups to stick together in the persistence of defiance to a teacher who is thought to wield coercive power unwisely so that the teacher is forced into the thoroughly untenable position of stooping to mass punishment which is manifestly unfair to fairminded adult observers outside of the group in question. Somehow, this leads to correction of intolerable situations when discovery by those in authority comes.

The withholding of a reward when it is believed to be due or earned is considered to be a cruel form of punishment. Nothing works more effectively to instil fear into students than to observe such behavior on the part of a teacher. The reasoning is to the effect that "if this could happen to others, it could certainly happen to me sometime." What then, started as a punishment for one, extends itself to the other members of the group, and in some instances, jumps the barrier of vacations and carries over to future classes.

What are some of the examples and forms of punishment visited upon pupils by teachers in an attempt to influence or change them in the direction dictated by the teacher? We have already mentioned the withholding of earned rewards. Actual physical punishment is one form of coercion which was formerly more in vogue than it is now, happily so. Perhaps the greatest single manner in which displeasure and punishment is visited upon a pupil is through low grades or failures, pointed critical remarks not of a constructive nature, and unusual and cruel assignments having little if anything to do with psychologically sound objectives and their attainment. The "busywork" technique is really a form of this coercion — buying peace and quiet for the teacher at the price of pointless application on the part of the students. One should distinguish between legitimate practice and necessary review and the indefensible busy-work sometimes given students just to occupy their time and attention and to "keep them out of trouble."

Holding a student up to scorn through ridicule is one of the worst forms of punishment. In the relationship which nominally holds, the pupil is powerless to retaliate at the psychological moment when such rejoinder would count the most. Fear, again the dread of consequences at the hands of the teacher, prevents a strong defense by the pupil. As teachers become more and more enlightened this practice of public or private ridicule is being reduced. Such practice hinders learning in the long run and is not a positive factor in the classroom situation.

One subtle form of punishment visited upon pupils by an otherwise good teacher is to give the impression that his present assignment to teach is not to his liking, that he is "stuck" with the class, that he really didn't want to teach this grade, or course, but actually preferred some other teaching assignment. Even the less intelligent pupils come to feel like an orphan who feels unwanted and unloved. Such a rejection of an entire class is not uncommon. Even if not a word is spoken to the class, it is painfully evident in the maneuvering of the teacher, the assignments, the testing, and the rigidity with which arrangements are made that the relationship is a strained one. It is also not uncommon that in situations similar to the one described above that the students in seeking their own protection may do a little punishing of their own with their teacher as the object of their affection. Such a position is really untenable for both sides to the controversy. It would have been better not to have permitted such a marriage of incompatibles than to suffer the tortures of a term before the welcome annulment is arranged. This is usually brought about merely by the passage of time and the end of the learning period.

Little if any values can come from the direct or indirect coercion of pupils. Inner desire to learn, self-discipline, pupil motivity, and willingness to expend necessary effort are prerequisites to learning. It is hard to scare a person into much profitable learning. So much of his time, thought and effort will be diverted and expended in the hatred, worry, fear and anguish that he will not be able to give his best attention to the direct application for learning. It is a shame to saddle youthful learners with such hindrances as pointless punishments.

What possible value could a student derive from conforming to group demands and teacher requests? In the first place, he might thereby secure rewards which would accrue for such action. In the second place, he might prevent sanctions or punishment in some form, such as rejection by both teacher and fellow students. The same might be said of such things as busy work or acquiscence in long, hard assignments. It is not so much what one could gain in an affirmative manner of speaking as what one could avoid in the negative sense. The rigors of learning are hard to bear when the steady diet is one of coercion. Just as the compulsions of the poor are indeed hard to bear, so too, are the compulsions of learners at the hands of any angry coercer. In the long run, the cost is self-respect for procrastinating, that is for forbearing to withdraw from the situation or starting a chain of events designed to overcome the major difficulty.

The by-products of coercion in the classroom are not hard to discover. Perhaps such action on the part of the teacher is in itself a by-product and comes out as misplaced aggression with the pupils as the only possible targets. After all, can such conduct be displayed at home, with fellow teachers, with the school administration? It wouldn't be safe, at all! With students, however, the by-products are unbelievable. The aggression escapes in out-of-class situations, at home, and perhaps is the fuse that lights unreasonable and unpredictable behavior for years to come. One has but to review some of the reasons related by aspirants for school boards and school faculties to realize that a "getting-even desire" has been festering for years and years. The by-products of hatred, resentment, premeditated malice, and ill-will are stored to the brim with students who have experienced such mis-education.

The power to punish is a dangerous one and should be used very sparingly if at all in the classroom. Teachers have lived to regret exceedingly such fitful outbursts which visited their wrath upon the innocent as well as the guilty. In one sense, however, the net effect of such behavior on the part of teachers is held lightly and rarely if ever exercised. In this way, pupils can develop greater respect for a teacher who holds great power but uses it intelligently. It must be remembered at all times that fear is the greatest single inhibitor of learning and that it ill-behooves a teacher to increase the grievous burden already borne by most young learners. The problem is great enough without extra emphasis being given to it. Actually, the powerful teacher will find ways and means of delivering a pupil from such dread weights so that his time and attention can be given over to learning of a profitable nature. The finest advice a pupil who is ridden with unreasonable fears can receive is how to understand and control such inhibitions. To be able to subdue such feelings, to avoid their drastic consequences, and to rise above them is the essence of the most powerful help a teacher can give a pupil. The practice of punishing for defects and limitations will not necessarily help overcome them. Surely the powerful teacher can find better approaches to extending his influence than to coerce responses from his students.

PRESCRIPTION POWER

Normally a teacher influences a pupil through an intentional, purposive, deliberate act as the social agent working for change. Action is here used to indicate the broad range of behavior on the part of the teacher among which is the physical presence of one who has been clothed with authority to prescribe behavior of students. This power to prescribe is legitimate in every sense of the word and it is so understood by all parties concerned with the educational enterprise. Pupils who do not concede that the teacher has such power and ought to use it have rejected the teacher-pupil relationship ab initio. And teachers who abuse their prescription powers have forfeited their privilege of being teachers as sooner or later the pupils will reject them and refuse to be influenced by them.

Growing steadily over the centuries has been the system of values held by mankind. One part of this set of beliefs and an awareness of merit has been the area relating to social deferment and the reasons thereof. For example, the appointment or election of a superintendent of schools clothes him with certain legal and traditional authority to carry out the purpose of his calling. Community leaders, teachers, pupils, parents and tax payers all recognize the soundness of the arrangement for to do otherwise would bring chaos in our social organization. Whether in law or in equity, roles have come to be defined in terms of their legitimate functions with power to match the responsibilities. Hence, parents wield powers of a wide latitude with respect to their children; corporation officials have been specifically granted authority by law to perform their duties; court officials are possessed of almost unlimited powers even to the taking of life of citizens for causes specified; and education officials have been delegated certain powers to accompany their endeavors in the classrooms of the nation.

It is when pupils do not understand and accept the fact that teachers have well defined powers to prescribe pupil behavior that they must be removed from the social situation for the good of the other pupils and the teachers. If they do understand and accept the teacher's role with attendant powers, then punishment is the proximate result of pupil violations. Some teachers feel that punishment in such cases is not as effective as education to overcome the deficiency. In cases where teachers attempt to exercise power which is not legitimate for them, pupils are fully justified in resisting their influences and refusing to change. In such cases the teacher engaging in such unwarranted behavior is reducing his over-all teaching power with his pupils as loss of confidence is the natural result of such ultra vires activities.

In simple cases of pupil acceptance of a teacher's power to prescribe, the basis for the power is outside of the teacher-pupil relationship at the beginning and derives from society's grant of such authority to the teacher. But as the power starts influencing the pupil, the center of the power moves back to the relationship developing between the teacher and the taught. Acceptance of the social structure is always a firm though temporary foundation for teaching power in the area of prescription. If pupils wish to take advantage of society's plan for educating its young, they must conform in major respects to the power figures appointed by society to govern the enterprise. Such legitimate power to prescribe is recognized and upheld in other social institutions, namely the family or home, the government and the courts, and the churches. To resist or reject authority of the school to prescribe behavior would ordinarily be frowned upon by other social agencies interested in upholding the entire social structure of which the school plays a key role.

In less structured teaching-learning situations, pupils voluntarily elect to come under the influence of teachers for the purpose of learning more than would otherwise be possible. Here such arrangements as tutoring, coaching, and other semi-class situations illustrate that individual learners actually desire to have their behavior prescribed with the hope that this will enhance their learning products. One can see the workings of such a voluntary power prescription in the joining of societies by pupils who thereby freely bring themselves under subjection of their officials and the rules of conduct.

What are some of the examples of the legitimate powers of a teacher to prescribe conduct of his pupils? The answer is a complex one for it involves other powers of teaching in a compounded situation. For example, when a teacher prescribes that a pupil shall "sit here" this may be exercise of the power to prescribe plus the power to reward or the power to punish as well as other factors or limitations. Generally, however, the power to prescribe is most obvious in the line of study assignments laid down from time to time, the work required on the part of pupils, the tests and examinations required to be taken, and the manner in which the daily activities are ordered. Little or no exterior interference is interposed in the classroom so long as the teacher appears to be reasonable and prudent in the exercise of the powers to prescribe. Some teachers welcome a type of higher prescription in the conduct of their professional work. This generally comes either from their own district superiors or from some country or state authority who specializes in specified areas. Then too, in some parts of the country, teachers and pupils alike find themselves at the mercies of periodic examinations which after a fashion dictate the spending of time and effort in an attempt to hurdle. Failure to negotiate this perilous passage of rating high on formal outside examinations prepared by competent authorities is grounds for withdrawing the power to prescribe. Generally, real prescription on the part of a teacher exceeds what is customarily required by the state and for which the teacher acts only as the simple agent in obtaining compliance. Failure to get compliance would ordinarily call for the employment of a replacement for the guilty teacher.

Just as the authority figures of the home, the church, and the state tend to re-inforce each other in the prescriptive power each wields, so too, the school and teachers tend to come into this picture. Resentful students of power plays in any area of life are likely to resent and fight against such tactics. The meek are generally the ones who accept without question the reality of the situation and go along with it. Breaking forth years later, however, it is sometimes discovered that reasons given for becoming prescribers in any of the fields mentioned above — family, religion, government or the school — is the stated wish to wield the power in a superior way to the way it was applied to pupils in years gone by.

There are approximately two million teachers teaching in American schools with another two million who prepared for teaching but are not now engaged in this endeavor. Of all the teachers who have ever taught, it would seem that most of them have not abused their power to prescribe. Mistakes of judgment have been made, and erroneous interpretation of their wishes have been reported by students, but by and large the power to prescribe behavior by teachers has been admirably handled. Perhaps one of the real reasons for this happy state of affairs is the great care with which society has chosen and commissioned candidates for the teaching profession. Other possible explanations might be that most public school teachers are females and probably employ maternal qualities in their work. Another possible reason is that teachers have so many first-hand observers and judges during the teaching process so that their every action is performed in the public arena — and of this situation, the teacher is eternally conscious.

The exercise of the power to prescribe by a teacher costs the student some of his freedom and liberty of action. However, this is more than compensated for in the additional gains in the direction of attainment of future goals at which time additional freedom will undoubtedly more than repay the pupil for his voluntary denial of an earlier period. Such temporary loss of freedom is not really much of a loss as the very young and even young adults have scarcely had time to value and utilize the vast amounts of time at their disposal. For children, play is about all the work they know; for older learners, it is still long before the time of responsible work assignments.

Nevertheless, students chafe under the restraints of school days. Even while physically maturing, they are receiving infantile directions, cautions, directives and what amounts to ultimatums with respect to their school work. From this they cannot escape. Whether at home or at school, the same steady diet of orders, directions, prescriptions, and advice comes without request. But somehow they endure it all and arrive at the stage of graduation which could more accurately be labeled emancipation from the prescriptive power of teachers.

While it may seem burdensome to both teachers and pupils, it is actually through this almost unlimited power to prescribe pupil behavior that the teachers has a chance of influencing the pupil during the learning time, and by developing interim understandings, attitudes, appreciations, skills, and acquiring knowledge may thus be able to extend his influence for eternity. For each pupil is changed in some way by having come in contact with each of his teachers.

IDENTIFICATION POWER (To Become Imitative)

The most awesome power of a teacher is his influence of a pupil to identify himself with the teacher through a mental process which may be and usually is subconsciously accomplished. It is a process of "becoming" for the student with the pattern of his ambition ever before him. This surely is one of the most potent influences on students who change even without being aware of it to become more and more like the teacher. A feeling of oneness develops on the part of the student even without the teacher being fully aware of what is happening or, for that matter, approving of the changes in his pupil. The attraction, close association, and a developing relationship of the two actors in this drama are enough to insure the extension of teaching power over the pupil. And so far as the pupil is concerned, the identification with his teacher is delightful if he is conscious of the change which is being worked in his life. In attempting to verbalize the situation, the pupil might reason that because he is in some respects like his teacher, therefore, he would naturally behave and believe as the teacher does, thereby insuring that he becomes increasingly like his ideal. The stronger the identification with a teacher, the more the student brings himself under the power of the teacher, thus actually seeking to learn what the teacher does believe, how he behaves, and even noting matters of dress and speech, patterns of ownership, and recreational ideas so that he, the student, can follow suit just as quickly as arrangements can be made, finances allow, or time permit. The transformation of a student into the image of his teacher thus becomes a prime example of a phenomenon of much interest to psychologists and psychiatrists.

As in the case of complex relationships between other forms of teaching power, we have also in this instance, another difficult situation. Where, for example, a teacher rewards a pupil in an ordinary situation, this might tend to develop the identification power at the same time. Punishment might be suffered gladly by a pupil who has identified with his teacher. In fact the identified might even seek ways and means of obtaining either rewards or punishments from the object of their affection — and all of this unconsciously. But since they are becoming more and more alike, the chances of violent disputes or disagreements are very unlikely as the pupil is prone to make great allowances for the behavior of his teacher thus setting for himself future permissive and limited behavioral outlets in a rationalistic pattern. The force of example now on the part of the teacher is likely to continue on for many years to come in the life of the pupil who has successfully identified with his teacher. Basking in the prestige of the teacher with whom he has identified, the pupil seeks ways and means of achieving for himself the same type of honor as his hero has received. The motivity of this type of teaching power is relatively unlimited and is likely to be passed on from generation to generation so that the influence literally affects eternity through succeeding generations of teachers and pupils.

Examples of a pupil's identification with a teacher may be found in pupils who develop their spoken English pronunciation, delivery, and sentence structure to approximate that of a favorite teacher. In matters of dress, there is great similarity. And if the teacher prefers to ride a bicycle, then so will his pupils who identify with him. If he prefers a small foreign car of a distinctive color, so will his pupils who look to him for the example. If he drops words of wisdom so will his admirers. Let him decide that he must have certain advanced graduate work or degrees and he will cause his following to scramble to do likewise. Should he author a magazine article or a book, the market will soon be flooded with fledgling attempts to write for publication also. If he is a bookworm, so they become if it is humanly possible. If a particularly colorful story comes from the great one, it will be cherished and retold for years to come as if it were a personal bequest to a favored son. Many of these players in the pageant look upon their teacher as a sort of spiritual father and give him honor as the one who, despite all others, really lighted the flame to real living and started the pupil on the road to real success.

Who can say that such strong influence as that described above is not a welcome and useful factor in the teaching-learning process? At least, it comes with enthusiastic desire on the part of the pupil for every little crumb which may be made available to him from the table of the master. There is an element of real danger in such a psychological situation, however, and it might seriously interfere with the future learning of the pupil who cannot with versatility switch from teacher to teacher as the case demands, or from school to school as the needs arise. Also, the personal element might come between the teacher and the pupil at a time when difficult though critical appraisals were necessary for the future progress of the student if he is to reach his potential. Examples of a teacher having to tell a student that he had taught him all he knew and that if he desired to continue his learning he must seek another teacher are rare. Yet they have occurred. Examples of pupils who openly brag about the teachers they have had and what their teachers have said about them as pupils and scholars are also known.

The whole theory of the protégé is probably an example of the value of this type of teaching power. Naturally, with such close supervision of the details of growth and development, the teacher becomes the coordinator, agent, public relations director, and father confessor of the pupil even when there are many other teachers charged with directing his learning in specific areas. In time, empire building is possible and very probable as a direct result of wielding this type of teaching power over a long period of time.

In terms of student costs for such a relationship of power to develop, one would think that it would be totally beneficial. This is not always the case. To compare all teachers against the one with whom one has identified will ordinarily be more of a contrast than a comparison, and certainly the hero of the situation will always be the one with whom one has identified. This is not to say that the others were not good teachers. Perhaps they were but the real and imagined benefits received from the favored teacher far outweigh the others' contributions taken together.

In terms of student benefits, they are probably incalculable. Borrowed courage, startling determination, unusual motivation, and dedicated sense of mission all come to the fore when a true identification has occurred. These qualities will ordinarily bring the pupil to the attention of his other teachers and will in due time bring rewards, attention, honors and opportunities. Knowledge of what the hero thinks of the pupil who has identified with him will also send the pupil into new or renewed activities to justify such faith and confidence. Should the title page of a gift book include some token of appreciation or prediction of success, these will spur the recipient into unusual attempts to completely justify the prophetic utterances of his hero. In terms of costs to the pupil who has identified with a teacher, it may be concluded that he has bargained for an unusual work output and a lifetime of effort to live up to his idealized reference.

The force of a teacher's power over pupils who have identified with him should never be underestimated nor belittled. It provides a driving force which cannot be easily stopped and is likely to be multiplied over and over again in the lives of other pupils who will identify with the identified.

EXPERT POWER (Acceptance)

A teacher's power over a pupil is in direct proportion to the pupil's belief that the teacher is an authority in the field. Such expertness would in probably all cases be judged against the background of the student's own knowledge and his knowledge of the specialization of others known to him. The former is a relative matter with the latter approximating an absolute standard of judgment. Influencing a student through the power of an expert reputation is easily accomplished. Even if it requires rejection of the views of parents, who are laymen, a child will oftentimes adopt the views and thereby be changed by a teacher's expertise in the area of the teacher's specialization. Further illustration of the point where one person is able to accept without doubt for the time being the word of an expert and act upon the information received might be of the parishioner who inquires of the pastor and follows the advice, a client who obtains information from his lawyer, a patient who relies on the guidance of his physician, and the stranger who seeks advice from a city dweller on directions and locations. In the case of the pupil who receives information from a teacher and acts upon it, he must surely come to look upon the source of such information as creditable and in the future have recourse to the same source. On the second or successive attempts, simple acceptance and reliance upon the information is usually observed. The teacher is extending his power over the pupil in cognitive realms. It is not customary for the pupil to consult the teacher outside of the realm of his specialization nor to permit the teacher to exercise power in any but the one area of narrow specialization.

The previous credibility of the teacher is important in the study of power of a teacher over a pupil. If the teacher has already demonstrated to the pupil the worthiness of the information to be received and acted upon on previous occasions, the pupil comes easily and quickly under the influence of the teacher on subsequent occasions. And if the pupil gets into the habit of unquestioned acceptance from the expert, his dependence on the teacher commences to grow and the teacher's power is thereby somewhat extended. As the student seeks to receive information only as clues to action instead of orders to action, then the independence of the pupil begins to assert itself and the power of the teacher over the pupil is thereby reduced even though the relationship still exists and is useful to some extent. If what a teacher says, believes, and teaches appears to fit what the student already knows about the subject, the teacher has very little chance of changing the pupil but merely of confirming him in the behavior already initiated. Should the communication not fit what is already believed about the subject, the pupil might reject any attempted influence of the teacher on an outright repudiation pattern, or conceivably if the teacher were considered a real authority in the field, repudiate his own previous understandings and espouse the position of the teacher thereby bringing himself under the direct influence of the teacher.

From the standpoint of society, the teacher is considered to be a subject-matter specialist and something of an authority within a narrow specialization insofar as his students are concerned. The concentration within one or more fields in the preparation for teaching and during in-service programs is usually sufficient to make the teacher as compared with his pupils the one in the group who knows the most about the subject. Perhaps he does not know more than many other teachers of his type and specialization, nor not nearly as much as state, national and international authorities in the chosen field, but at least he is in close contact with his pupils who are seeking to learn from him. Actually, the pupils have access to all of the authorities in the field through their teacher and the recorded knowledge indicated in the course of study which is under the direction of their teacher. It is the case of the bird in the hand versus better birds in the bushes so far as the pupils are concerned. And so far as their parents and the school authorities are concerned, their teacher is the best expert or authority in the area that the school could afford — or at least this is the assumption.

In the case of an authority located at the school but not teaching classes in which a pupil is enrolled, it is still very possible that power could be and often is exerted widely on the students across the district or campus. Through the chain of command, channel of communication, circles of friends, and other avenues, recourse can be had for organized information, opinions, speeches, and other expressions of expert knowledge on which students can base their actions. It is always possible that the one exercising the power is not even acquainted with the one being influenced and changed.

It has been pointed out that even the non-believers are influenced by an expert to some degree even as his opponents seek to undermine his position and prove him in error. Such activity may be traced to indirect influences and as such come under the heading of the power of an expert to influence both of his friends and foes alike. While it is of little or no consequence at all, many fervent discussions are heard about the positions of specialists as if the swirling debates could in some way influence the expert. Innocent questions asked of an authority sometimes lead to his further thinking and the amending of sections of his views and organized reports.

In connection with the subject-matter specialists employed by society to work with the young, it should be pointed out that, far from being authorities in the field, these teachers look upon themselves as being users of the works of specialists and mediators of the culture rather than as the leading exponents of authoritative points of view from the standpoint of the experts. Regardless of this modest self-classification, students tend to regard their teachers as the first real authorities in the area of academic subject matter to rank with lawyers, doctors, and religious leaders as experts in the areas in which they have chosen to practice.

Barring a clash of personalities, or tendency to unfair administration of the teaching-learning enterprise, most students welcome the power of teachers along the line of specialization as time saving and of personal value in explaining and interpreting what other and perhaps higher authorities have said about the subject under study.

The delayed effect of some of the teaching power in the area of specialization and expertness has become obvious to many students who have gone on to other schools and other instructors only to find that in former situations the subject was carefully and powerfully taught. Unrecognized at the time, and for an intervening period of time, the realization at last arrived that the influence of a former teacher had taken hold in a most powerful manner so as to either change or make change more difficult in the days ahead. Some students even return to the scenes of earlier education hoping to recover the relationship and build again the type of effective control once enjoyed.

It has become customary to refer to the power of ideas rather than the power of idea givers. However, this may be, the donor should receive the credit for wielding the influence when the idea refuses to remain inert but enters into the life of a pupil and with force and power changes his whole life and widely influences the lives of all those who come in contact with him through the idea. For how do we separate the speech from the speaker, or the thought from the thinker in such situations? The deed and the doer reflect the power of the teacher who prepared the student for such action.

Chapter 6

Theories of Teaching Power

There are many elusive facets to the subject of teaching power. Throughout the study there have been points on which there was not enough tangible evidence or thinking to warrant a position at the present time. To assist in pointing up the areas in need of further study and research, this chapter contains specific formulations of statements relating to teaching power. While they are all listed as theories, many of them would now appear to be beyond that stage.

In the following pages, after the statement of the theory, a few words of explanation or elaboration are given leading to questions which seem to be unanswered at the present time.

1. *Teaching power is a function of and based in the fluctuating relationship of teacher and learner as modified by the pressures of other human relationships.*

In a normal, characteristic manner, the power of a teacher over a given student is believed to be based in the personal relationship, which obviously must be cultivated if it is to grow and become strong. If it is neglected over a period of time, it would be natural for the relationship to languish. Such a relationship is not a one-way affair but increases in strength as mutual efforts are made to build it. While it should be understood as a person-to-person association, it must also be admitted that many modifications are forced into the particular relationship by other human beings who have an impact upon it because of their insistent needs and pressure for teacher attention for themselves.

As a theory of the basic source of teaching power, much more research should be conducted in the wide area of human relations and personnel management to provide additional insights and understandings into the psychological foundations of educational relationships. Some of the specific questions to be answered might be: What causes automatic acceptance of a teacher's authority by some while others reject it ab initio? Why do some pupils develop a strong teacher-pupil relationship almost from the beginning while others never do, or at least get off to a late start? Is it possible to develop wholesome teacher-pupil relationships if the teacher-pupil ratio remains at 30 to 1, or 25 to 1 or 20 to 1? Are the relationships stronger in groups of pupils of 15 or less? Is the 1 to 1 ratio ideal and all others reduced in their relationship effectiveness because of the quantity factor?

2. *Teaching power is best and can only be demonstrated in terms of growth and development in relation to understood goals.*

If this theory contains any merit, such procedures as asking teachers to rate themselves on their own effectiveness can at best be only indirect, make-shift ruses. A more defensible procedures would be to devise ways and means of measuring pupil growth and development in relation to understood goals and let such reports throw light on the power of the teacher to influence their lives. Teacher nor pupil promotions, teacher nor pupil popularity, teacher tenure nor salary would be taken into consideration in testing the theory that teaching power can be demonstrated only in relation to understood goals. The goals would then provide the yardstick against which the growth could be checked. This would probably force some type of understanding of goals at the beginning of the teacher-learning process so that directions and milestones could be established for later possible use in demonstrating the power of the teacher. Testing such a theory would also undoubtedly call for a careful assessment of the past learnings so that these could be excluded from the current period of measurement. Research along this line might well take into consideration whether the goals were teacher goals or pupil goals; whether the growth and development would have occurred without the teacher contribution; whether there were differences in pupil growth and development between the sexes; whether the growth and development were uniformly achieved or came in spurts; whether the ones who made the greatest progress were the ones who had ostensibly developed the closest teacher relationship; and whether pupil growth and development is accompanied by an awareness of such on the part of students and teacher. One might also speculate that goals developed on a mutual or joint basis might be superior to those laid down by the teacher for the use of pupils.

3. *Teaching power is increased by intensive study of the human elements involved in the relationships in order to understand conditions, needs, directions, associations to be dealt with.*

This is not so far-fetched when one considers that this is very true in the fields of law and medicine. The teacher who aspires to wield maximum influence in the lives of his pupils will give much attention to the study of their conditions, needs, directions, and associations. What clues are to be found in such a study will be extremely useful in the day-to-day conduct of instruction and the guidance function supplementing teaching. An experiment might be conducted where the teacher remained aloof from the pupils and did not seek to familiarize himself with the information mentioned in the statement of the theory. Another study of say another section of the same class might be made where the teacher conducted an intensive study of the human elements involved in the teacher-pupil relationship. Comparison of results in terms of teaching influence on a short term basis could then be made. It probably will be discovered also that wherever students study the human qualities of their teacher from the same points of view as those recommended for the teacher's study of pupils, that the learning power of pupils is enhanced greatly.

4. *Teaching power is demonstrated in student lives in overcoming weaknesses, developing strengths, resolving problems, and satisfying personal needs in socially acceptable ways.*

From the standpoint of immediacy, such a theory makes good sense. From the long-term point of view, however, whatever the teacher does today in terms of teaching must wait for longer periods of time to find expression in changed behavior. For it takes time to overcome weaknesses, develop strengths, resolve if not solve problems, and to satisfy personal needs in socially acceptable ways. And teachers know this even if pupils do not at the present time. After the teacher's work is done, the pupil will oftentimes if not usually, have to work out his own salvation. This is what is meant by the application theory in education. It is one thing to acquire cognition and another to go beyond such understanding into the deeper area of actual application and use in a personalized, specific manner. It is the latter which is proof of the demonstrable power of the teacher even though both teacher and pupil must wait months, and even years, for such fruition to occur. Research might be conducted to provide light on the desire of students to overcome their own weaknesses as seen by others as compared to weakness of which they are aware; whether need satisfaction in socially acceptable ways is facilitated by students or resisted by them; whether the teacher is the only one desiring to overcome defects in the lives of pupils; whether pupils believe teachers have either actual or potential power to help pupils with their real problems; whether the content of school courses plus the activities of the school address themselves to what students consider to be their problems and needs or whether they feel that such proffered help is artificial and not appropriate at the moment. A teacher who desires to increase his teaching power will never be content to miss the boat, not even with one pupil, and will explore every legitimate means of helping his pupils in the areas of their real and pressing concerns.

5. *Master teachers are presumed to possess substantially more teaching power than other teachers.*

The word "Master" is not intended to limit its descriptiveness to holders of the degree by that name. Recognition of past teaching power would seem to warrant designation of a teacher as a master teacher. Upon what criteria are master teachers chosen? Is possession of the degree in and of itself proof of teaching power? Do pupils of master teachers have opportunities to learn that pupils of other teachers do not have? What are the qualifications of a master teacher? Will experience lead to the development of teaching power and the truly descriptive title of "Master Teacher"? Should beginning teachers identify master teachers and seek to emulate them in their teaching techniques? Will employment of the same or similar procedures used by master teachers bring a beginner to the same status of Master Teacher? How do master teacher. Upon what criteria are master teachers chosen? have master teachers secured? Is there something in the personality of a master teacher which is missing from other teaching personalities? Do master teachers have better teacher-pupil relationships than do other teachers? Are pupils or parents able to identify teachers with great teacher power potentials? Are school administrators able to spot master teachers prior to their employment? Are fellow teachers convinced that a teacher who has been designated a master teacher is, in fact, one?

Teachers as a lot are modest. Few if any will take credit that does not belong to them and some are even so modest that they will not accept credit for what seems to belong to them. One usually finds teachers are not the ones who sponsor "Teacher of the Year" or even "Outstanding Teacher" awards but that this usually comes from outside sources at least in its inspiration and promotion. The whole area of "master teachers" needs much more attention than it has ever had.

6. *More than elaborate exercises and precepts for achieving teaching success are needed for generating and developing teaching power.*

There is something quite impersonal about following a formula for developing teaching power. Precepts from above are not so successful either. Perhaps a teacher who really wants to be a good teacher, who has the native ability, and who is deliberately working toward that goal will find ways and means of achieving that purpose. Mass rules on the subject however simple would not seem appropriate or even advisable. There are so many factors beyond the control of the teacher to be taken into consideration on this issue that it may not even be fruitful to engage in research and experimentation on it. However, some of the unanswered questions surrounding the area are: Will following the letter of a rule produce the desirable results of improved teaching or must the teacher somehow possess the spirit and other intangible qualities to follow in the footsteps of recognized and outstanding teachers? Will imitation of master teacher activities provide a teacher with the sure means toward more powerful teaching? Would following meticulously the points in a teacher rating scale, consciously attempting to rate high on each one, provide a sure avenue to teaching power? Libraries of pedagogical directions, criteria for improvement, golden rules of education, statements of competency, definitions of good teachers, psychological commandments for teaching, and the like are already available for teachers. Is there any evidence that their use can or ever has increased teaching power?

7. *The design for teaching power must necessarily be worked out on a personal basis in terms of experience, style, planning and purpose rather than on administrative fiat or supervisory requirements.*

If schools, or teaching are not as good as they could be, are they going to improve very much just because it is so ordered? Why is it that within a given school plant, one teacher will be recognized as a very superior teacher whereas others are known to be either "average" or in some respects, inferior? Has not the administration desired better than this? Or is it helpless? Is a move toward more powerful teaching doomed if it is laid out on a mass basis, patterned after an order from the top that will force conformity on all below? Is the quality of teaching such a delicate commodity that it must be designed on an individual basis in terms of the one teacher's apperceptive mass, his current determinations, his own personal style, his opportunities to make progress? Is a design for increasing teaching power very similar to designing a life's career? Can it be mass produced so that it fits all and sundry? Who is able to counsel or advise a teacher who truly desires to move forward in his quest for personal improvement as a teacher? Do the generally understood social provisions for more formal schooling, perhaps while in service at nights, week-ends, summers, and during leaves qualify as an adequate design for increasing teacher power? Do the school board incentive plans for acquiring more formal credit appear to fall within a design for developing more teaching power for pupils under the jurisdiction of the board?

8. *Teaching power is not evidenced by indoctrination or use of propaganda tactics.*

This is power of another sort. Propaganda, in a perjorative sense, contemplates getting others to believe or do things they would not otherwise do if they were in possession of all of the facts. For this reason, the propagandist is usually very happy to arrange the flow of information so that if it is believed, a predictable result will be obtained. The power of a propagandist is in many respects just the opposite of the power of a good teacher. For example, a powerful teacher will insist upon all of the relevant information, that is, both sides of an issue will be considered, whereas, the propagandist lays out the facts which cause pupils to arrive at the conclusions desired by the propagandist. Perhaps, the pupil is not aware of the process at work and falls prey to such miseducation. To believe that a teacher possesses great power when he doesn't is not necessarily harmful but it is a curious commentary on teaching as such when the very opposite result can be obtained than that universally desired. That poor teachers can be considered good by administrators or boards, or by themselves, is preposterous but sometimes true. That powerful teachers can be considered poor by pupils, teachers, administrators, parents, and boards is abominable. Yet this situation may exist. One thing is sure: Teaching power is not evidenced by indoctrination or use of propaganda tactics in the worst sense of the term. Wherever such procedures prevail, one should suspect just the opposite of powerful teaching in the positive sense.

9. *Clearly understood purposes and firm intentions on the part of the teacher are necessary for teaching power.*

There is a growing body of literature on the subject of the uses and abuses of objectives in the classroom. Are goals really important to teachers and pupils in the classroom? Can it be possible that even with elaborate lists of stock objectives for given school courses and areas, many teachers and pupils are able to all but ignore them and carry on with little or no attention given to them? Do they ignore objectives at the risk of reducing what otherwise might have been more powerful teaching and more productive learning? Is it really necessary for a teacher to have "firm intentions" with respect to a class, or an individual, or the subject-matter of the course, or any other feature of the teaching-learning situation? What is the effect of attempting to teach a class without clearly understood purposes and firm intentions on the part of the teacher? What is the effect on pupils if they discern that their teacher has no such clear understanding or firm intentions? Is it possible for pupils to learn very much in a class situation which is not marked by clearly understood purposes on the part of pupils as well as the teacher? Is it true that he who teaches least teaches best?

10. *The sine qua non of teaching power evaluation is specific and clear understanding of the teaching objectives.*

On what basis would or could a teacher evaluate the work of pupils if the teacher did not have a clear understanding of the teaching objectives? Or to what would a comparison be made down through the years after the instruction had been given? It should be noted that not only should the teacher and the students know what the teaching-learning objectives are, but the theory enunciated above goes on to make such knowledge and understanding essential to anyone who seriously attempts to evaluate the teaching power at any time. There are those who might claim that a pupil in say 1975 might be compared with himself back five or ten years before and thus avoid any reference to the teaching objectives. Comparisons and contrasts of this type could be made but would the results reflect any evidence at all on the power of the teacher? If on the other hand, the instructional objectives were definite, the teaching-learning process were concluded, and the lapse of time had intervened, and then it was found that the pupil had indeed exhibited behavior held up before him as desirable goals during his earlier learning period, it might provide some evidence of teaching power.

11. *Teaching power can be indirectly assessed by an examination of the quality and quantity of the general products of pupil learning which have been inventoried as understandings, skills, attitudes, and appreciations.*

Is such an assessment more likely to reveal power or force? Is the teacher entitled to credit for all of the achievements on the part of his pupils? Is there any way to separate credit due to former teachers, to parents, to the pupil himself? Would it be a valid judgment to say that a teacher has great teaching power just because practically all of his students had indeed gained understandings, skills, attitudes, and appreciations in abundance during the year he taught them? Would not another measurement need to be made a year or even five or ten years later to be sure that the earlier judgment was in fact justified? Is compulsion or force when exerted on pupils and when it results in high achievement, the proof of teaching power? By "indirectly" is it assumed that whatever is shown on an early inventory of skills and other learning products will probably continue on down through the lives of the learners and thus reveal teaching power at a later time? Must a period of time elapse so that the one who attempts to gauge teaching power will have perspective and incontrovertible proof of lasting influence stemming from prior instruction? Is it really possible to estimate the quality of an attitude or take the count of appreciations to such an extent that credit for their development can be given or responsibility fixed? Is it really possible to check on the teaching power of a teacher while the instruction is in progress?

12. *A report on a teacher's power could be shown by inventory of the six elements of teaching.*

With reference to the Edman aspects of teaching, which divides teaching into understanding pupils, preparing materials for them, presenting the materials, evaluating the results, re-presenting if necessary, and reporting on the achievements as a matter of useful knowledge and record, this theory holds that a teacher's power might be divisible by six and that it might be low in one of the six, high in another and so on. Is it possible that a teacher could have great teaching power in presenting materials of instruction without even understanding his students, their problems, and their individual needs? Is it possible that a teacher could have great influence on students in the area of testing, measurement and evaluation and yet have little or no power in the area of communicating interpretations of such test results? Are there teachers who are such good subject-matter specialists that their first love is to the field and not to their pupils? If such be so, is it possible that in preparing materials for instruction, their power is great, but that in presenting them personally to students, they are very poor indeed? What a complication we get into in considering the possible application of this composite theory! And yet, it may be that until research and experimentation have worked out some of the details of the above questions we shall continue to talk about teaching power as if it were indivisible and a single entity when actually it consists of a cluster of discrete and not so discrete abilities.

13. *Peer group influence (power) competes with, complements, and supplements a teacher's power so that credit or responsibility must in most cases be shared.*

Even if it is commonly reported that the teacher is credited for exerting the greater influence on a pupil, it remains to be proved that the peer group's contribution of providing a reinforcing situation, and incidentally introducing a note of competition to add greater motivation, has not substantially altered the teacher's part in the educational process. Shared credit and responsibility is, beyond a doubt, a fact of academic life. As to whether a teacher's influence meets competition from the pupil's peer group, again, there seems to be little doubt. As a theoretical proposition, it seems quite plausible that a teacher's influence on a given pupil finds some complementation, supplementation and competition at the hands of the peer group.

The degree of teaching power possessed by a teacher would seem to be reflected by the degree to which he arouses his pupils to take initiative, direction and control in their own self-instruction. This is certainly an extension of the multiplier effect that a powerful teacher possesses.

14. *Teaching power is and should be shared among the principal contributors to the learning enterprise, i.e., parents, peers, and pedagogues.*

To this list could be added others and such agencies as the home, church, state, the press, as well as schools. It will be noted that education in its broadest concept is here intended and not schooling in a narrow sense. Agency personnel bear responsibilities for education in varying degrees. The school normally acts as the enterprise coordinator in the absence of strong family direction. If the team wins, no one player should then have all the glory.

15. *Individual disciplinary situations reflect a low degree of teaching power for the given pupil.*

Presumably if the child or student is in trouble, academically speaking, then the teacher has not exercised enough power to help overcome the experienced difficulties. Neither has the team jointly provided the preventive maintenance necessary to keep the learner functioning in a trouble-free manner. For the record of powerful teachers is clear: the situation is soon transformed into a pattern of security and success, especially if the insecure and unsuccessful are susceptible to the teacher's influence to any marked degree. This does not at all deny that a troubled student does not influence both his classmates and his teacher or teachers. It goes without saying that many students have been delayed in their own learning by other students who did not want to learn nor did they apparently wish others to learn. Teachers have actually resigned their positions and left the profession because of incidents and difficulties falling into the category of disciplinary situations. To yield to such a temptation is but to admit lack of power to cope with the bad situation. Defeated in the here-and-now leads inevitably to denial of powerful influence in the future. To substitute force for the real elements of teaching power ordinarily will not effect the changes desired by the teacher. Force is so fleeting in its influence that little or no residual deposit of power remains for later assessment.

16. *Teaching power is likely to be increased and promoted when due regard is given to activities appropriate to clearly understood teaching and learning objectives.*

There is at least a presumption what when the teacher and pupils engage in activities in line with worthy objectives, that is to say, the activities which are psychologically sound, then there is a likelihood of increased teaching effectiveness both in its short term results and long-term influences. One might wonder about situations where teacher purposes were not clearly understood by pupils, or where in fact, not closely related to their learning objectives. The maximum opportunities for powerful teaching to occur would seem to exist when there is general harmony prevailing between the teacher's proposals and the pupil's proposals, perhaps not at first, but sometime soon after the teacher-pupil relationship is established. If the two principals are at cross purposes, then the teaching-learning process will be about as ineffective as it is possible for it to be with mutual attempts at extinguishment of the adversary's intentions and plans. There would seem to be no substitute for clear vision toward an agreed-upon goal of instructional achievement.

17. *Teaching power cannot be measured; at best it can be evaluated by studying teaching indirectly, that is, examining its results which are classified as products of learning.*

These products of learning have been listed by writers on the subject as skills, understandings, attitudes, and appreciations. When one is listening to how much a given teacher has influenced a person, it seems perfectly patent that the area being described is the one covered by the term "products of learning." It must always be remembered that no teacher can do the learning for a student and that there is no royal road to learning. Any one of the products of learning must come as a result of the teacher's efforts, the pupil's efforts, the learning media, i.e., all the bits of information, rules, laws, theories, facts, ideas, ideals, and other means of solving problems. To attempt to measure the media of developing the products of learning, or to look closely at the teaching-learning process itself, or to assess the amount of information received by learners would be obviously self-defeating if one were to attempt to measure teaching power in that way. Power relates to the results not the means. The importance of knowledge has always been identified with its use so that the old maxim of "Knowledge is Power" has been revised to read "Knowledge, when used, is Power." So that in the thesis proper, the statement indicates that the products of learning offer the best means of evaluating teaching power, there is much evidence to sustain the position if it be understood that use or demonstration or application of the products of learning (skills, understandings, attitudes, and appreciations) will be forthcoming. And with this, there must needs be the lapse of time to provide opportunity, perspective, and the fixing of credit or responsibility for the learner's total performance subsequent to the time of learning.

18. *One key to teaching power is the strategic and tactical use of appropriate potential subject matter.*

If a differentiation is made between actual and potential subject matter with the latter already acquired but not yet used or applied in a profitable manner, it seems reasonable to assume that the teacher who helps the learner to hoard much potentially useful subject matter might in time become thereby a more powerful teacher than the one who did not have the foresight to counsel along this line. Obviously, the teacher who can assist in acquiring potentially useful subject matter and who can follow this up by making it absolutely mandatory to use what has been learned will in time become more powerful than those teachers who find no ways of teaching application. The world is full of those who can read but who won't or at least don't. Likewise it seems to some that there are many who can think deeply and rigorously but who appear to be reluctant to do so, choosing the easier course of relying on others for this service. The powerful teacher does not indeed stop with the acquisition of subject matter by his students, whether it is actual or potential in nature. This is but the good beginning for which the lifetime of usage remains. The powerful teacher stresses the intelligent use of subject matter in attacking all manner of problems. This is why some who have lived closely with persistent problems feel that the method of problem solving is far more significant than simply acquiring more facts. Not only how we acquire subject matter, but how we plan to use it and put the plan into effect falls under the heading of methodology. Stated differently, a knowledge of subject matter as such is not sufficient but rather only partly enough; the knowledge and will to use subject matter intelligently in the solution of human problems is just as important and without which the first situation would be almost entirely without significance.

19. *Teaching power is reflected to some marked degree not so much in ability to do but in doing without reluctance.*

Those who learn what and how to act but who are reluctant to act are not as productive nor as effective as they might be. The teacher who, for one reason or another, assists in the development of a young person whose attitudes, appreciations, knowledges and skills lead him to this half-educated behavior, must face the decision of history. Somehow, someway, teachers of power find ways and means of shaking their students out of lethargy; firing them up to new heights of endeavor; lighting an eternal flame of active, creative discernment; giving a sense of destiny and man's present opportunities to help shape the forces controlling him. There are, no doubt, plenty of teachers who could perform more effectively. The mystery is not hard to fathom of why they do not. Somewhere in their background of experiences, there was never developed the desire for such eager spirit. Call it a philosophical shortcoming if you will, or explain it in terms of psychological structure, but the fact remains that there is a reluctance to perform up to capability. When detected, the powerful teacher should make this weakness the first order of business in the overcoming of it on a permanent basis.

20. *Teaching on any one or all three of the levels — elementary, secondary, and higher — is not as good as it could be.*

For years, it was said that there were cases of over-achievers in our schools and their opposites, the under-achievers. It has always seemed difficult for educators to understand how a person could overachieve but there is almost agreement on the problem of under-learning and achievement. The capacity of a person to teach would seem to be an iron-clad limiting factor in the development of teaching power. The problem, however, relates more directly to those who have the capacity but who are under-achievers. The question of proof remains a major obstacle in this problem. Is it ever possible to prove that pupils could have learned more than they did? Or that a teacher's influence could have been more extensive?

21. *Teaching power should precede teaching responsibility as one is not justly held accountable for events unless he has the power to affect them.*

This, one might suppose, could constitute the whole theory of certification of teachers by some agency, usually the state or other political unit. To certify to the public that the holder possesses the power to teach is a reasonable interpretation of the legal theory of certification. In this sense it is a protection to the using publics to have the teacher possess evidence of teaching capacity in the form of a written certificate issued by competent authority. One might also suppose that the issuing authority over the centuries has been notably lax in examining into the qualifications of the teacher to exert substantial influence on his pupils. The usual rule have been to require evidences of attendance at school for given periods, satisfactory passage of courses of study with specified credits, along with other attributes. Possession of good physical and mental health, having reached a given age and other requirements do not at all testify to teaching power. Perhaps, though, these qualifications come close to advising in a negative way, that the certified teacher might possess potential teaching power as certain negative rules had been met already. These so-called negative requirements might be illustrated by rules against having communicable diseases, not being a criminal, not being a Communist, not advocating overthrow of our government by forcible means, and the like.

A teaching readiness doctrine with some application and interest might be that the main task of instruction is to make ready for whatever the pupil intends to do in the future.

In a sense, capacity to teach is certified by a government agency before the possibility of taking on the responsibility of teaching is permitted. But this capacity is necessarily pegged at a minimum standard of preparation for teaching whereas the concept of teaching power contemplates the optimum if not the maximum contribution.

22. *Testing is a key to the evaluation of teaching power.*

If by testing is meant the measuring of amounts of subject matter pupils master during the course of instruction, there is grave doubt about the usefulness of the theory. But if the long-term view is taken to mean the performance out-of-school and throughout life is to be weighed, then the theory makes immense good sense. The word "testing" of course must be understood in the broader concept of trials, performances, and the proving situations so realistically common to us all except in schools where the problems are not quite real, the testing is somehow artificial, and the attempts to permit pupils to prove themselves all falter someway in the area of consequences. Attempts to describe the school as a simplified society and to discount the chances of young people getting hurt while getting an education all refer to the artificiality of paying the price for the mistakes we make while in school. Eventually, however, all barriers are removed and we as free human beings write our own records of successes and failures with all the in-betweens. This type of testing would seem to be the key to the evaluation of teaching power.

How can we check on teaching power? Will well-designed subject matter tests at the beginning of a learning period, in the middle, and at the end provide enough feedback on the instruction in time to do any good? Would follow-up studies be the answer? Such questions, while seeking to find a way, point to a mostly irrelevant position.

23. *Research is the key to teaching power development.*

Here again, in the narrow sense of institutional research, pure research, or basic research, the theory makes little or no contribution to the understanding of teaching power. But the type of research which permits a teacher to get to the bottom of problems of everyday school teaching such as the understanding of the pupils in depth, the understanding of what subject matter and media for its presentation are available, the skills needed with which to plan intelligently with pupils for their own education, and such other so-called action research techniques, all these should prove immensely valuable in the development of teaching power in a given situation.

24. *Prospective teachers can develop teaching power through imitation of teachers who have already become powerful.*

This is an interesting position and one which might lend itself to some form of further study. It has been suggested that an important tip on increasing teaching power would be to get straight-thinking and sound-reasoning teachers to demonstrate daily routines on how to think and reason effectively. Students could then imitate their well-educated teachers. Skillful communication of all types should be stressed so that the most effective routines can have maximum carryover values. The substance of this theory is that teaching power is not taught by words but by actions and demonstrations of power by teachers of teachers and would be an eminently practical way of developing teaching power.

25. *Higher salaries will ultimately bring greater teaching power as the public demands it and rewards it.*

The old chicken-and-the-egg controversy of which comes first has its counterpart here. On one side of the issue are those who say if and when teaching power is demonstrably present, the higher salary recognition will follow quickly as a reward and in order to insure its continuation. On the other hand, it is charged that without higher salaries first, the teacher is in no position to develop the power of which he was capable. Furthermore, adherents of this line also charge that the body of teachers must first be financed in order to increase corporate teaching power. The alternative to this, it is asserted, is to allow only a very few to achieve positions of eminence by reason of their significant achievements. Has this been the verdict of history?

26. *Capacity for adaptation is the prime source of achievement of teaching power.*

Of this there seems to be little doubt. Still, in the language of the rebellious, non-conforming teacher who works to destroy the passive spirit of conformity and false adjustment to the fictitious status quo, the powerful teacher is the ubiquitous gadfly of bold enterprise. In one sense, however, the capacity for adaptation is basic to the very existence of life itself. An understanding of this "law" and the wise engineering of changes in the personal areas of life could conceivably contribute much to effectiveness in teaching. Compromising and adjusting to the conditions of life as they are today, however, seem very wrong to the powerful teacher, who with courage and determination strike forward for the goal of maximum development of the individual. Instead of the individual adapting to his environment, the powerful teacher is helping the pupil to do just the opposite.

27. *To have teaching power, a teacher must possess professional mobility.*

One can understand that a powerful teacher might and very likely would have mobility, and that a mobile teacher might have power. On the other hand, a notoriously unsuccessful teacher might have been mobile for years with frequent position changes. Whether the theory contemplates the relationship of power and mobility in a causal or consequential framework is problematical. The theory is an interesting one. Examples of display of great teaching power without in fact having much mobility undoubtedly could be found. Those with mobility have not necessarily demonstrated teaching power though many have done so. In times of teacher shortage, mobility tends to increase without, one might judge, an accompanying increase in teaching power.

28. *The record of teaching power is spelled out in the long run by the consequences of choices teachers and students make or accept.*

Take for example, the selection of subject matter by a teacher for his students. Knowledge today comes from a seemingly inexhaustible reservoir and the task of the selecting teacher is not only difficult but urgent as well. While it has been said that if a task is important it is not really urgent and vice versa, it appears that the teacher who would exert substantial and maximum influence on his pupils might find exceptions to the rule. Choosing the media for change is not an easy task for a single teacher but surely calls for the teamwork of professional colleagues and the cooperation of all segments of the school's many publics. Furthermore, it is not a simple task to determine which knowledge is of most worth in the present, to say nothing of the near impossible task of prophesying about its value for many years into the future.

Many there be who aspire to greatness in teaching but few are ever recognized as such. Could it possibly be in the singing language of the poet that "many a gem of purest rays serene the dark unfathomed caves of ocean bear?"

29. *The teaching profession has too lightly taken its responsibility for effective teaching and too readily allowed itself to hide behind the seeming conflict of mass education and excellence.*

For centuries, schools and teachers have endeavored to exert a powerful force in the battle for the progress of mankind. No profession can afford to be without the perspectives and motivations of insight and foresight nor to allow its basic science to become so abstract as to ever lose its present relevance. There is danger of teachers becoming and remaining passive with respect to their own competence while awaiting and expecting researchers to provide all the answers to their professional problems. Passive conformity with watchful waiting has too often been a criterion of professionalization as viewed by some. Others, in defense against such tactics prefer an open, direct confrontation of the personal and situational factors tending to hinder or prevent the most powerful teaching of which a person is capable. The necessity for action — immediate participation by the teacher — is obviously a criterion for teaching power. Preparation for action is the essence of potential powerful teaching performance. Myriad substitutes for effective teaching action characterize the ineffective practitioners who deviously embellish their rationalizations over perceived weaknesses. It must be evident to most discerning professionals that teaching power must be sought; it cannot be imposed. The would-be powerful teacher prepares the soil for greatness of and for his pupils. Tilling the grounds of scholarship, planting the seed ideas, and watering with encouragement are the inspired tactics of the great teacher. Simply doing the "right things" will never suffice. Psychology, with all its concentration on motivation and the dynamics of living, could be immensely helpful to the teacher who aspires to be highly influential with his students. Further exploration of the contributions of a knowledge of psychology needs to be made. The same claim could be made for philosophy, for history, and for the language arts of reading, writing, speaking, listening, as well as the non-verbal methods of communication.

30. *The claim has been made that the art of effective teaching is founded on psychological facts discovered by the scientist.*

Perhaps so. In a period characterized by real need for improvement in the greatest single enterprise in the world, education, the quality of teaching-learning assumes important new dimensions. Teaching is and always has been a dynamic, evolving profession. This is so partly because the needs it strives to meet are themselves constantly changing. Not surprising then is the factor of the changing teacher in many respects, hopefully of course in the direction of increased teaching power, but not always so. If this thesis is to be sustained and teaching to assume its place in the sun, more and more of our teachers will necessarily have to become scientists in the sense used by Woodruff as he refers to the art of creative or effective teaching. They will have to discover facts for themselves. Research in the field of psychology is increasing rather steadily. If the thesis is to prove useful, teachers will need to study psychological reports regularly in order to perfect their art and science of teaching toward maximum teaching power.

POSTSCRIPT

It has been alleged that, through public demand, the teaching profession is in the restaurant business, the banking business, the transportation business, and the entertainment business. These are certainly important related and necessary services in many parts of our country. To teach, however, simply means to make to know how. The archetype of teaching is not based on such peripheral activities however necessary and worthy as the ones listed above, but upon skill in helping learners help themselves through the power and ability of a teacher to influence his pupils. Naturally, a deep understanding of the teaching-learning process is a firm requisite for teaching power. Some, including teachers, have all but lost sight of this real reason for the school's existence. We need to be reminded constantly of one of the profession's most persistent problems — that of quality, excellence, and power in instruction.

Teaching is like learning to cook. It cannot be done by simply studying a recipe book. The need for a more thorough approach to preparing potentially powerful teachers is acute. It would be in order, in these times of frantic searching for more powerful members of the teaching profession for the major professions in our society to join hands in an intensive, extended, on the job, scientific assessment of the efficacy of the procedural arrangements, techniques, devices, tactics, and methods used in obtaining candidates, screening them, and in the effective education of prospective lawyers, doctors, preachers, bankers, law enforcement officials, labor leaders, military leaders, engineers, career diplomats, dentists, railroaders, aviators, telephone company workers, industrial managers, oil industry leaders, and the specialists from the ranks of the motion picture, radio, journalism, theatre, and public relations areas. Many practical ideas and suggestions for more powerful teaching exist within these disciplines and occupations. After all, they are a little closer to the realities of adult life and the problems of their clientele because their clients have already achieved adulthood, while the teaching profession works mostly with the young where reactions and adjustments seem to come less rapidly. Within teaching ranks, during the past half century, have come successive waves of interest and activity in such important professional areas as scientific testing of intelligence, achievement, and personality, ability grouping, curriculum making, novel administrative schemes, and minor movements in methods of teaching. All such activities wrought their improvements in the overall outcomes of instruction. Also during this period, the country has had successive "new" this and that to occupy the attention of teachers and parents. From new psychology to new arithmetic, the schools have gone from one field to another. In a sense, the past fifty years have been very similar to an exercise "bootstrap" in which the profession is trying to elevate itself. There have been great professional strides since 1947 with the leadership coming from various groups within the organized profession. Millions of Americans agree with the philosophy of the educational leaders that what teachers can do to improve themselves, particularly with reference to teaching power, they must do, and do quickly.

While the public will probably always retain and exercise the right to tell schools what to teach, it will continue to leave the methodology of teaching to the profession. There is a need, however, to demonstrate publicly, all the time, technical, professional competence leading to the accurate judgment of the American people that their teachers are powerful influences in the lives of their students.

A serious search for better ways of teaching will focus attention of the entire profession and the country on the problem of teaching power. Changing times have brought the profession many new factors to complicate the formal educational process for which teachers are mainly responsible. New avenues of coordination of home, church, state and school activities will and should be discovered. As these better practices become understood and widespread, thousands of professional teachers will be able to increase their teaching power.

Teaching is emerging with renewed vigor from a long period of painful reconstruction in the hope of becoming a true profession. It faces tremendous challenges in the social, political, and economic areas. The basic challenge, however, would seem to be coping with the internal problem of the quality of teaching. If this could be settled, perhaps the political, economic and social victories would follow swiftly. The time has come for teachers to rise to the challenging opportunity of increasing their teaching power by imaginatively attacking the many complex problems of instruction that beset them. Clearly, the quality of teaching is not as good as it could be; clearly the growth of teaching power capable of achievement is not at a desirable rate; and clearly, there seems to be no policy of encouragement to more rapid development of potential teaching power. But the drive, flexibility, imagination and desire are all available. How soon and how well we provide leadership for the development of teaching power in the mother of the other professions will indicate the fundamental progress in American education.

Powerful teaching can institute a permanent revolution in the lives of those who come in contact with it. It is highly threatening to the status quo, does not inordinately dwell upon the past, but looks to the dawning of a brighter day ahead.

Notes

Chapter 1

1. NEA Research Memo #1962-17, NEA Research Division, National Education Association of the U. S., May, 1962, p. 7.

2. School and University Program for Research and Development, Harvard University, 1962, p. 3.

3. John W. Gardner, "Impact of Change on Education," *Panorama,* World Confederation of Organizations of the Teaching Professions, Winter Issue, 1960, p. 28.

4. Herbert Spencer, *Education* (New York: D. Appleton & Co., 1860) p. 48.

5. From a Report of the White House Conference on Education, 1955, p. 99.

6. National Citizens' Commission for the Public Schools, "How Can we Get Enough Good Teachers?" 1953, p. 55.

7. Quoted from pp. 7-11 in Evaluation of Student Teaching, Twenty-eighth Yearbook, Association for Student Teaching (Lockhaven, Pa.), State Teachers College, 1949.

8. "Men must be taught as if you taught them not, and things unknown, proposed as things forgot." Line 15, Part III, "An Essay on Criticism," by Alexander Pope. From *Eighteenth Century Poetry and Prose* by Louis I. Bredvold, Alan D. McDillop and Lois Whitney (New York: Thos. Nelson and Sons, 1939), p. 352.

9. Harold D. Lasswell, *Power and Personality* (New York: W. W. Norton & Co., 1948), p. 10.

10. Elias Canetti, *Crowds and Power* (New York: The Viking Press, 1962), p. 281.

11. Harold D. Lasswell, *Power and Personality* (New York: W. W. Norton & Co., 1948), p. 21.

12. Harold D. Lasswell, *Power and Personality* (New York: W. W. Norton & Co., 1948), p. 18.

13. Floyd Hunter, *Common Power Structure* (Chapel Hill: University of North Carolina Press, 1953), p. 2.

14. Sir William Blackstone, *Commentaries on the Laws of England* (Chicago: Callaghan & Company, 1884) Cooley's 3rd ed. Revised, Book I, p. 453.

15. Bernard I. Bell, *Common Sense in Education* (New York: Wm. Morrow & Co., 1928), p. 176.

16. Frank Jennings, "Great Teachers," in *Toronto Education Quarterly,* 1:16-17, Summer, 1962.

17. Quoted from *The New Dictionary of Thoughts* (New York: Standard Book Co., 1936), p. 151.

18. Nathan Marsh Pusey, *The Age of the Scholar* (Cambridge: Harvard University Press, 1963), pp. 68-69.

Chapter 2

1. Thomas H. Briggs and Joseph Justman, *Improving Instruction Through Supervision* (New York: The Macmillan Company, 1952), pp. 161-169.

2. See California Statement of Teaching Competence for listing of roles, pp. 20-24 of Chapter 4.

3. Edward B. Weisse, "Five Steps To Quality Education," *The Clearing House,* Vol. 38, Nov. 1963, No. 3, pp. 158-60.

4. Frank A. Butler, *The Improvement of Teaching in the Secondary School* (Chicago: University of Chicago Press, 1939), p. 66-138.

5. N. L. Gage, *Handbook of Research in Teaching* (Chicago: Rand McNally & Company, 1963), p. 479.

6. Ralph K. Watkins, University of Missouri, Emeritus Professor of Education.

7. N. J. W., "I Taught Them All," *The Clearing House,* Nov. 1937.

Chapter 3

1. Roger H. Garrison, *The Adventure of Learning in College* (New York: Harper & Brothers, 1959), p. 161.

2. Richard L. Turner, *Journal of Teacher Education,* September, 1963, p. 306.

3. Fred M. Hechinger, "The Missing Yardstick," The New York *Times,* Sunday, July 9, 1961, Sec. 4, p. 8E.

4. Department of Classroom Teachers, National Education Association, Discussion Pamphlet No. 10. (Washington, D. C.: The National Education Association, 1954) p. 5.

5. Edgar L. Morphet, Roe L. Johns, and Theodore L. Reller, *Educational Administration, Concepts, Practices, and Issues* (Englewood Cliffs, N. J.; Prentice-Hall, 1959) p. 361.

6. Emery Stoops and M. L. Rafferty, Jr., *Practices and Trends in School Administration* (Boston: Ginn and Company, 1961) pp. 427, 431-2.

7. Chester T. McNerney, *Educational Supervision* (New York: McGraw Hill, 1951) p. 121.

8. Nelson L. Bossing, *Teaching in Secondary Schools* (Boston: Houghton, Mifflin Co., 1952) 3rd ed., pp. 246-7.

9. Gordon Allport, *Measurement of Teaching Style,* A handbook for College Teachers, edited by Bernice Cronkhite (Cambridge: Harvard University Press, 1950), p. 45 ff.

10. *Ibid.*

11. Jack V. Edling, from the September, 1962, *Journal of Teacher Education,* pp. 346-353.

12. Luella Cole, *The Background of College Teaching* (New York: Farrar and Rinehart, Inc., 1940), pp. 558-561.

13. Howard M. Jones, *The Idea of a University Once More,* p. 94.

14. University of Chicago, 1953, Diagnostic Reports on Comprehensive Examinations. See B. M. Bloom and D. R. Kratwohl, *Taxonomy of Educational Objectives: Handbook I, The Cognitive Domain* (New York: David McKay Co., Inc., 1956).

15. Association for Higher Education; College and University Bulletin, Vol. 17, No. 11, March 15, 1965, p. 1.

16. John E. Stechlein, "How to Measure Faculty Work Load," American Council on Education, 1961, p. 1.

17. N. L. Gage, *Handbook of Research on Teaching* (Chicago: Rand McNally & Company, 1963), p. 425.

18. Edgar W. Dale, *Audio-Visual Methods In Teaching* (New York: The Dryden Press, 1946), p. 39.

19. Edward Lee Thorndike, *The Psychology of Learning, Educational Psychology* (Teachers College, Columbia University, 1913), Vol. II, pp. 1-5, 54-56.

Chapter 4

1. Harvard Law School Handbook for Entering Students, Harvard University, p. 21.

2. School and University Program for Research and Development, 94 Prescott Street, Cambridge 38, Massachusetts, 1951-1962, p. 3.

3. Carl R. Rogers, "Personal Thoughts on Teaching and Learning," *Improving College and University Teaching,* Vol. VI, Winter, 1958, No. 1, p. 4.

4. B. I. Bell, *Common Sense in Education* (New York: Wm. Morrow & Co., Inc., 1928), p. 173.

5. Nathan M. Pusey, *The Age of the Scholar* (Belknap Press, 1963), pp. 15 and 168.

6. Roger H. Garrison, *The Adventures of Learning in College* (New York: Harper & Bros., 1959), pp. 170-171.

7. Ralph W. Tyler, *Basic Principles of Curriculum and Instruction* (Chicago: University of Chicago, 1950) pp. 4-28.

8. Ralph K. Watkins, *Techniques of Secondary School Teaching* (New York: The Ronald Press Co., 1958), p. 15.

9. Frank A. Butler, *The Improvement of Teaching in Secondary Schools* (Chicago: The University of Chicago Press, 1954), pp. 29-163 and 265-340.

10. Association for Student Teaching, 28th yearbook. (Lockhaven, Pa., State Teachers College, 1949), p. 7-11.

11. Stephen Corey, "Action Research To Improve School Practices" (New York: Bureau of Publications, Teachers College, Columbia University, 1953).

12. John Dewey, quoted in *The New Dictionary of Thoughts* (New York: Standard Book Company, 1936), p. 75.

13. *The Salina Journal,* August 12, 1964, p. 4.

14. Jack V. Edling, *Journal of Teacher Education,* September, 1962, pp. 346-353.

15. Frederick Mayer, *Creative Universities* (New York: College and University Press, 1961), p. 89.

16. Clarence F. Birdseye, *University Administration* (New York: Baker & Taylor Co., 1909), p. 39.

17. Paul Douglass, *Teaching for Self-Education* (New York: Harper and Brothers, 1960), p. 17.

18. Nathaniel Cantor, *The Dynamics of Learning* (Buffalo: Foster & Stewart, 1946), p. 47.

19. Winslow R. Hatch, "The Lecture," The Improving of College and University Teaching. (Corvallis, Ore.: Oregon State University, Winter, 1958), p. 21.

20. The National Education Association, The Education of Free Men (Washington, D. C.: The National Education Association, 1941), pp. 109-110.

21. William M. Alexander and Paul M. Halverson, *Effective Teaching in Secondary Schools* (New York: Rinehart & Co., 1956), p. 63, 66.

22. Fred C. Ayer, *Fundamentals of Instructional Supervision* (New York: Harper & Brothers, 1954) p. xiii.

23. Kimball Wiles, *Supervision for Better Schools* (New York: Prentice-Hall, 1950) p. 76.

Chapter 5

1. Elias Canetti, *Crowds and Power* (New York: The Viking Press, 1962), p. 387.

Index